THE GREAT COMMISSION AND YOU

Disciple-Making in Daily Practice

Endorsements

"It is a delight and honor commending this groundbreaking work by Stan Cook. We live in a day with a surplus of great resources for all dimensions of discipleship, yet we still find emaciated believers and frustrated spiritual leaders. Particularly in the shadow of a pandemic, economic and social upheaval, and increasing hostility and indifference toward Christianity in the West, clarity and focus on discipleship matter more than ever. As one of the co-developers of the Discipleship Dynamics Assessment ™ used in this work, I am very encouraged by Stan's integration of this tool with the realities of creating new pathways of growth for the local church.

Thinking in terms of outcomes and allowing programs to serve the outcomes is revolutionary, and this work is an excellent window on changing the culture of discipleship in the local church. Though Stan's particular project focused on two dimensions, the whole person was always in view. I hope this work finds a wide readership, and more importantly, serves as a call to action to reimagine discipleship for a new era of gospel impact. Offering the people of God a clear vision of 24/7 flourishing and then being able to measure and adjust the pathways of equipping is a gift to the church and the world. I commend this work to all spiritual leaders and serious followers of Jesus. In God' providence, it is one part of a coming awakening."

— Dr. Charlie Self
Director of Training, Made to Flourish
Visiting Professor, Assemblies of God Theological Seminary
Co-Developer of The Discipleship Dynamics Assessment ™

"Having been privileged to follow Dr. Stan Cook from his formative years in Bible college to his mature stage of doctoral studies in seminary, I assure you that he has been a faithful disciple whose authenticity has been demonstrated in his making disciples of new generations of Christ-followers during his pastoral ministry (2 Tim 2:2). Now, with this book, Dr. Cook has blessed the Church with a biblically grounded, practical handbook that will facilitate the work of other pastors, lay leaders, and congregations in refocusing and fulfilling the paramount purpose of Christ's Body on Earth."

—David R. Bundrick, M.Div., Th.M., Ph.D.
Asst. Professor of Bible and Theology,
Southeastern College (1981-86)
Academic Dean, Assemblies of God
Theological Seminary (2013-2015)

"The Church must turn from event driven strategies to discipleship paradigms. Covid compelled change. You get what you celebrate. Let's celebrate lives transformed! Let's be intentional. Dr. Cook has delivered a home-run work for five-fold leaders. God is shifting wineskins. Is He shifting yours? This book is not for the shelf. It's for the desktop. You'll find yourself pulling from it daily if you're in church leadership! Five stars!"

—Joseph S. Girdler, D.Min.
AGTS D.Min. Cohort 30 Ministry Colleague
Superintendent-Kentucky Assemblies of God/USA
Friend

"Dr. Stan Cook's book is a breath of fresh air. The call and plan for discipleship is rooted in biblical truth and not diluted by modern dogma. The text is well researched and not full of conjecture. I foresee this book becoming a valuable resource for the local church."

—Dr. Adam C. Sikorski
Associate Professor
College of Church Leadership, North Central University

"The Great Commission and You: Disciple-Making in Daily Practice is a unique offering to help the church understand and navigate the importance of missional discipleship. As usual, my father gets to the heart of the matter. The church has drifted off its course from the core mission, disciple-making, and the Great Commission. Fortunately, this book helps direct our way forward in a clear and digestible way."

—Caleb Cook
Author's Son

THE GREAT COMMISSION AND YOU

Disciple-Making in Daily Practice

Foreword by
Rev. Scott Brown

Dr. Stanley Cook

Dedication

To Heidi,
lifelong friend, partner, mother of my children,
and warrior in Christ.

Contents

Foreword

It is my privilege to introduce Dr. Stan Cook, who has faithfully served the kingdom of God along with his wonderful wife, Heidi. I have felt the quality and authenticity of this couple at every engagement. I vividly remember walking away from them the first time we shared a meal together and thinking how refreshing it was to hear someone passionately resolved to the idea that the church was more capable, more empowered, and more equipped to change the world than it is realizing in America. Each subsequent conversation did not disappoint. I had met a man who was not going to be satisfied with the status quo of a one-hour weekly class or Bible study being passed off as true biblical discipleship. Here was a man who would not accept a program or watered-down definition of discipleship to rob the church of its God-given potential.

Stan's passion is that the church recaptures the biblical truth that every child of God is called to be a disciple-maker as part of the Great Commission. One cannot separate discipleship from evangelism, prayer, worship, fellowship, occupation, family, relaxation, or any part of one's life. If you are looking to refresh the status quo or plan to do the same thing and hope for different results, then this book may not be for you. If you desire more, though, and are willing to examine your own actions against that of Scripture, Stan's insights will be a breath of fresh air.

—Rev. Scott Brown
Ordained Minister with the Assemblies of God

Preface

Jesus called the disciples, and they left everything to follow Him. He taught them, trained them, and showed them how to be His disciples and how to make new disciples. His final command to them was to make disciples wherever they went. Today, however, the command to become disciples and make new disciples appears to have a watered-down meaning. Yet the call to becoming a disciple has a clear, biblical path for believers to follow, and following that call is a must.

This book explores how disciples should mature throughout their spiritual journey. The content in this book came about as a result of my doctoral research, which involved developing teachings related to sixteen outcomes identified by the dimensions of spiritual formation and personal wholeness in the Discipleship Dynamics Assessment. From my biblical-theological research, I developed lessons presented in a weekly classroom structure to benefit my congregation. The weekly sessions underscored the assessment and brought to light the need for whole-life, discipleship practices.

Adapting this material for a broader audience will make these principles available not only to individual believers in devotional study but also for local church ministry in such areas as small groups, classroom settings, leadership training, and preaching ministry.

May God bless you as you continue to allow His Spirit to form you spiritually and bring you to a place of personal wholeness.

Acknowledgments

Life is a journey. On my doctoral journey, I experienced many different adventures, side roads, hills, and valleys. My journey to the Assemblies of God Theological Seminary (AGTS) was an adventure to say the least. From my first conversation with the admissions department through the final edit of my D.Min. project, I found myself humbled and grateful—humbled that God would lead me to this remarkable institution of higher learning and grateful for the phenomenal faculty and staff who poured into my life and believed in me.

So many assisted me during the project part of my journey. My Cohort 30 mates who led the way and got there before me inspired me. My project adviser, Dr. Charlie Self, assisted me throughout the process and encouraged me to pursue the study of discipleship. My D.Min. biblical adviser, Dr. Doug Oss, provided valuable theological support for my chapter 2. My project coordinator, Dr. Lois Olena, was patient, kind, and exhibited qualities of 1 Corinthians 13! Thank you for encouraging, pushing, prodding, and dragging me across the finish line. I appreciate Hanna Lyons' help as well; she is the best editor in the world!

Thank you to my friend and co-conspirator in the disciple-making journey, Pastor Scott Brown. Scott and Debbie opened their church and hearts to allow me to pursue this project. It was an honor working with you. I am grateful for the Trinity Chapel Assembly of God family who participated in my journey. Your willingness, grace, and insights were invaluable.

I have been blessed to have a family tree filled with pastors, teachers and evangelists. My childhood overflowed with Bible stories, hymns, and tales of service to Jesus and transformations of souls. My grandparents—Stanley W. Cook and Evelyn E. (Cook) Bibler as well as Charles and Peggy Clere—were pastors, church planters, and lovers of Jesus. They walked with God down paths that most would fear to tread. Thank you for your faithfulness. To my siblings, Ron (Becky), Renee (Scott), and Cheryl (Kevin), endured my doctoral journey with patient endurance and inspired me. My mom, Myra Church, instilled in me a love for Jesus, His Word, His people, and His world. She has always been an example of Jesus that I attempt to replicate in my life.

To my wonderful children, Katelyn (Caleb), Caleb (Erin), Jacqueline (Josh), and Abigail (Jacob)—you are my world. My favorite job is being a dad, and you have made it easy! To this day you continue to inspire me with your love for others, your compassion, your work ethic, and your love for Jesus! Also, many blessings to you for my grandchildren: Allison, Benjamin, Silas, and the many more yet to be born.

To my heart, Heidi. You are my sunshine on a cloudy day. You endured with patience and love many years of me writing papers, reading books, and developing projects. You graced me with the greatest gift I could receive in life: a lifelong friend, partner, mother of my children, and warrior in Christ. I could not have done any of this without your encouragement.

To my Savior and soon coming King who has forgiven all my transgressions and transformed me, thank you for loving me and calling me to be your disciple.

Introduction

When Jesus commanded his disciples to "go and make disciples of all nations" (Matthew 28:19), he spoke the mission statement for the church. Jesus told his disciples to do what he had done during his three years of ministry. Jesus made disciples by selecting a few into whom he poured his life" —Greg Ogden[1]

The Great Commission is the command given by Jesus to His followers at the conclusion of His earthly ministry. This command has been followed to various degrees by the Church universal in subsequent centuries. As time has passed, the Church has placed more emphasis on process, liturgy, and institutional programs than on the act of making disciples. The call to follow Jesus is a call to "be enlisted as disciples within the Christian community, whose reception of the Christian message in faith must be actualized in their lives."[2] Disciple-making is an intentional act. It is not merely a downloading of information about Jesus but putting into practice what Jesus taught. Eugene Peterson explains that "A disciple is a learner, but not in the academic setting of a schoolroom, rather at the work site of a craftsman. We do not acquire information about God but skills in the faith."[3] The Great Commission requires learning but also requires action on the part of believers.

This book provides an opportunity for believers to go from learning about discipleship to practicing the life of a disciple. Putting the knowledge and action together will help develop a whole disciple who lives the life Jesus calls the disciple to live.

The Great Commission Jesus gave His disciples in Matthew 28:19-20 exists as the standard for believers to follow. "Go and make disciples" (v. 19) remains the command that should underscore and determine all believers think and do.[4] The knowing, doing, and passion of the Great Commission, however, provides a dichotomy of understanding in both knowledge and implementation.

The biblical understanding of Jesus's words and the modern understanding are often in sharp contrast. Jesus called the disciples to action. His command was to make disciples of all nations. This was to be achieved as the disciples were going. They were to baptize and teach new disciples to obey all that Jesus commanded. The modern Church has slipped into program-oriented discipleship that requires only the amount of effort it takes to keep the program going. The relationships required to make disciples are replaced with attendance at a church function or class.

The modern Church has slipped into program-oriented discipleship that requires only the amount of effort it takes to keep the program going.

Greg Ogden points out three critical issues in disciple-making: (1) disciple-making is about relational investments, (2) disciple-making is about multiplication, and (3) making disciples is a transformative process.[5] The modern church needs to renew the biblical ways of making disciples.

There exists, then, the opportunity for deeper comprehension and appreciation of the biblical teaching of the "doing" of the Great Commission. A disciple-making church presents the occasion to bridge the understanding between knowledge of and acting out the Great Commission with the passion that the good news brings. The opportunity exists to ingrain the discipling DNA in believers through every means possible, including such specific, measured means as this project.

I trust that this book can help pastors and other ministry leaders to mobilize believers for a process of embracing a whole-life discipleship model that produces disciples who make disciples. When I first became aware of the Discipleship Dynamics (DD)[6] tool to help promote whole-life disciples while doing my doctoral studies, I learned about the thirty-five biblical discipleship outcomes and five domains of a holistic approach to discipleship: Spiritual Foundations, Personal Wholeness, Healthy Relationships, Vocational Clarity, and Economics and Work. The scope of this present book will address only the first two of the five dimensions of Discipleship Dynamics: Spiritual Formation and Personal Wholeness.

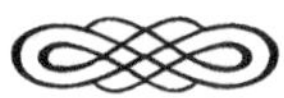

The need for the modern Church to assess its disciple-making process and make the necessary adjustments is vital to the future of the Church.

The book is in three parts:

- **Part One** presents the biblical-theological foundation of the book—examining the biblical mandate for discipleship in the Great Commission of Matthew 28:18-20, and then examining the concept of discipleship across the Old and New Testaments.

- **Part Two** considers the professional literature with respect to the heart of discipleship, how disciple-making takes place in church practice, and the nature of whole-life disciple-making in terms of the two dimensions of spiritual formation and personal wholeness.

- **Part Three** provides practical helps for pastors and church leaders to walk through these principles and practices with their core leaders, ministry teams, and congregations. These materials may also be adapted for personal/devotional use by individuals.

The biblical concepts of disciple-making and discipleship are the primary command Jesus gave to the disciples and the Church. The attention the early Christian disciples gave to this command helped change the world. The need for the modern Church to assess its disciple-making process and make the necessary adjustments is vital to the future of the Church, as Paul Tanner, in discussing the Church, states:

> "Comfortable Christianity" is the siren seductively luring us to crash on the rocks of personal ruin. A wasted life with nothing to show for itself is a sad fate, especially if prompted by a sense of shame for Christ and his words. If we truly value our lives, we would be concerned for what we have to gain for all eternity, not merely for what we can have in this world. Discipleship is costly—Jesus said so![7]

Disciple-making must become more than information and attending a church service. It needs to be the focus of the church with actions that allow others to see Christ. Disciples will do well to follow the command of the Great Commission. The world needs disciples who make disciples.

PART ONE

Any attempt to define *discipleship* in one abbreviated definition results in a myriad of possible outcomes, the results of which tend to be drawn more from church tradition or meaning than from a biblical description. That is not to say that church traditions and definitions are derived from other than biblical sources. It merely means that the modern Church has allowed itself to become enamored with traditions and meanings to the detriment of true biblical discipleship. M. Rex Miller notes that discipleship is not a class or small group but instead "a lab project, a choreographed dance, an art taught under the eye of a master. It is apprehended first through demonstration, not intellectually."[8] Discipleship is more than a class or a downloading of information. Discipleship is about relationships. It is about people.

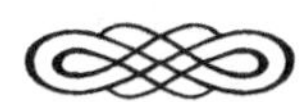

Discipleship is more than a class or a downloading of information. Discipleship is about relationships. It is about people.

Biblical discipleship implies wholeness, hence the usage of the term *personal wholeness*. In following Christ, the disciple is made whole and is being made whole. Charlie Self explains this more fully by identifying that

> Christian discipleship must be fully informed by biblical wisdom that unites faith, work, and economics. Neither the ancient Israelites nor the New Testament Christians would have separated the "practical" and the "spiritual" or the "personal" and the "social," as so many do today.[9]

Biblical discipleship stretches the believer beyond the

meaning of the biblical term for *disciple* (*mathetes*) which in simplified terms means "learner." Michael Wilkins asserts that "this overemphasizes one aspect of the term's meaning and misses what the term primarily signified in the New Testament era."[10] He continues on to say, "A disciple was one who made a life commitment to a particular master and his way of life."[11] This commitment encompasses all areas of a disciple's life.

Jesus's call to His disciples is the call to make more disciples (Matt 28:19-20).[12] This command has become known as the Great Commission. Followers of Christ are to go into all the world and make disciples. This was not a foreign concept to the first-century followers of Christ. Being a disciple (or follower, learner) of a master was a known concept in the first century. However, "Jesus' disciples were not to choose another master, or become masters themselves. Instead, Jesus' disciples were told to go and make disciples of the nations—to teach them what Jesus had taught them."[13] The understanding of disciple was known, but the command was fresh and decisive. Andrew Dragos notes, "The life of discipleship was anticipated in the Old Testament, made explicit in the Gospels, and fleshed out in the Epistles and other New Testament writings."[14] The concept of discipleship permeates the Scriptures from Genesis to Revelation.

The Biblical Mandate for Discipleship:
The Great Commission

The *Great Commission* is a descriptive term used by the modern Church. Timothy Tennent explains the Great Commission "is a relatively late expression used to refer to the final commission of Jesus Christ to His disciples."[15] He further adds that this expression first appeared in print in 1899.[16] As this phrase has increased in usage, it is imperative that the followers of Christ fully understand the meaning and its applicability.

Matthew 28:18-20

Matthew's Gospel concludes with what is known as the Great Commission. In Matthew 28:19-20, Jesus instructs His disciples to "Go therefore and make disciples of all nations, baptizing them in the name of the Father and of the Son and of the Holy Spirit, teaching them to observe all that I commanded you. And behold, I am with you always, to the end of the age." As Craig Keener notes about the significance of the placement of the Great Commission, "The Great Commission is not an idea tacked inelegantly to the end of Matthew's Gospel, as if Matthew had nowhere else to put it. Rather, it summarizes the heart of this Gospel's message."[17] The Great Commission is at once the culmination of Jesus's earthly ministry and the inception of the ministry of the disciples to the world. Matthew 28:18-20 is the inspired completion of Matthew 1:22-23: Jesus is the With-Us-God! Disciple-making is the invitation for others to know this dwelling of God.

The words of Jesus to His disciples begin with a declaration: "All authority in heaven and on earth has been given to me" (Matt 28:18). Jesus holds all authority. As R. T. France explains, "Of course Jesus already had authority during his earthly ministry. But now he has all authority, and that word all will be repeated insistently in vv. 19 ('all nations') and 20 ('all things', 'always')."[18] This echoes Daniel 7:14 concerning the surety of the

The Father has given His Son all authority on earth. It is in this authority that the disciples can take the gospel into all the earth.

Son of Man that "to him was given dominion and glory and a kingdom, that all peoples, nations, and languages should serve him; his dominion is an everlasting dominion, which shall not pass away, and his kingdom one that shall not pass away."[19] In the Great Commission then, as Craig Blomberg states, this brings the reader to the conclusion of Matthew in which

> Jesus is passing the torch to his disciples, even as he promises to be with them forever—spiritually, not physically— to empower them for future mission. Jesus can make the claim of v. 18 only if he is fully God, inasmuch as the whole universe is embraced in the authority delegated to him.[20]

The Father has given His Son all authority on earth. It is in this authority that the disciples can take the gospel into all the earth.

The central command of the Great Commission is for disciples to make more disciples (Matt 28:19-20). Turner and Bock point out the significance of Jesus's first word of this commission: "therefore." "It is crucial to note that this verse begins with 'therefore.' The point is that Jesus, having been exalted, was now in a position to send his disciples forth in mission. Their mission is possible because Jesus is potent."[21] The disciples are sent, by the power of Christ, not only to the Jews but into all nations.[22] And the purpose of going into all the world is to make disciples. Wilkins posits that the Great Commission:

> …contains one primary, central command, the imperative "make disciples," with three subordinate participles, "go," "baptizing," and "teaching." The imperative explains the central thrust of the commission while the participles describe aspects of the process. These subordinate participles take on imperatival force because of the imperative main verb and so characterize the ongoing mandatory process of discipleship to Jesus.[23]

Following the central declaration of Jesus becomes the focus for the disciples thus depicting this as a mandatory command rather than an optional suggestion.

Matthew uses the term *matheteuo* (to make disciples). This is the third time Matthew uses this verb (13:52 and 27:57). Wilkins records that the first two occasions have a passive tone: "has become" or "has been made." "Here the verb takes on a distinctively transitive sense, 'make a disciple,' in which the focus is on calling individuals to absolute commitment to the person of Jesus as one's sole Master and Lord."[24] To become a disciple is to make a life commitment to Jesus.

Notice that the command is to make disciples with the emphasis on the making of the disciples rather than on the "go."[25] Making disciples of all nations requires that some disciples go into foreign lands to proclaim the good news. But the emphasis the church has placed on the "*go* and make disciples of all nations" (emphasis mine) has contrarily led to the de-emphasis on "making disciples." Hahn summarizes that, "Though almost all English translations render the word **go** as an imperative, it is a circumstantial participle in the Greek text. A most literal translation would be 'When you go, make disciples.' The commission of the Church is not simply to go; going is assumed."[26] Therefore, the beginning of the Great Commission could be stated, "As you are going," or "When you are going," make disciples of all nations.

The concept of being a disciple was common in the ancient world. Nässelqvist explains that "In the Greek world … a person became a disciple as he sought out a teacher and followed him and his principles. Similarly, in the rabbinical tradition, a 'learner' or 'student' attached himself to a rabbi or to a movement."[27] This type of discipleship is dependent upon the master and his teachings. Disciples would follow a master's way of life, adjusting according to the teachings. When Jesus called His disciples, they may have understood the call to be similar to what was already known.[28] Paul Helm submits that, "The calling of these disciples took place at a time when other teachers had their disciples, most notably the Pharisees (Mark 2:8; Luke 5:33) and John the Baptist (Matt 9:14)."[29] The disciples Jesus called were willing to follow Jesus and learn from Him in the traditional sense.

To be a disciple of Jesus is to be called to make new disciples. Hans Kvalbein points out "the evident implication of the Great Commission. … The disciples are told to make disciples. The concept of 'discipleship' is a dynamic concept."[30] The norm of becoming a follower of a master now transitions to a new norm: being a disciple who makes disciples. Wilkins adds that "Jesus took a commonly occurring phenomenon, discipleship, and used it as an expression of his kind of relationship with his followers."[31] He further states, "Jesus

To be a disciple of Jesus is to be called to make new disciples.

patiently taught his disciples what it meant for them to be his kind of disciple, his kind of follower."[32] The master-student relationship that the disciples had known, Jesus changed. It was this shifting relationship on which Jesus began to focus.

Jesus's Model for Making Disciples

The scene of Jesus walking around Jerusalem and the surrounding areas followed by His disciples is a familiar one in the Gospels. Wilkins identifies "That vision of discipleship demands our attention, both on an historical as well as a personal level."[33] It is during these scenes that the concept of discipleship is instated. Paul Tanner notes, "Jesus is defining the terms of discipleship (what it means for a believer to follow him), not giving instruction on how to become a believer."[34] The disciples discovered that Jesus's discipleship methods require more than sitting at the feet of the master to learn. Robert Webber explains how Jesus, "Instead, following in the tradition of Hebraic holism, … taught that becoming a disciple is a process that takes place in the continuous way in the worship and community life of the church."[35] His methods involve living more as an apprentice studying the work of a master.[36]

The bond between Jesus and His disciples was distinct.[37] They were hand-picked by Jesus to be part of a group. This is the model Jesus established for them to follow. Following Jesus would not be easy and was not meant to be done alone.[38] Greg Ogden explains the importance of personal connection by identifying that "The scriptural context for growing disciples is through relationships. Jesus called the twelve to be with him, for through personal association their lives would be transformed. Proximity produces disciples."[39] Having called His disciples, Jesus made a practice of spending time with them.[40]

In the time Jesus spent time with His disciples, He taught

them and trained them. As Russell Huizing notes, "Jesus took a band of relatively untrained individuals and within a short period had qualified them to lead his mission to change the world—which they promptly began to do."[41] Modeling discipleship by building relationships, teaching, and then doing were part of what made Jesus successful in His endeavor. Jim Putman identifies three keys to Jesus's success as the greatest disciple-maker in history: (1) Jesus was an intentional leader in every sense, (2) He did His disciple-making in a relational environment, and (3) He followed a process that can be learned and repeated.[42]

There is a cost to being a disciple of Jesus. A disciple is called to give up one's own interests to follow Jesus. As Lilly notes, "The first group of disciples, along with their amazing success, experienced much affliction, deprivations, and suffering. In the end it cost all but one of the disciples their lives."[43] Jesus placed high demands on His disciples. He demanded loyalty, self-denial, an aptness to learn from Christ and teach what has been learned. He gave them authority as His spokespersons and power to perform signs and wonders.[44]

There is a cost to being a disciple of Jesus.

Five Main Ingredients

Bill Hull notes that Jesus used the Pharisees as an example of how not to disciple others. Matthew 23:1-7 explains why their methodology was hypocritical and selfish. The Pharisees preached but did not practice what they preached. They placed heavy burdens on the people but did not lift a finger to help them. They loved the place of honor and rejected the humility of service. Hull explains that "Jesus taught the power of humility in spirit and submission in community. This is the way to get transformational traction, to practice a faith that transforms."[45] He adds that adopting the five characteristics "of a first-century disciple, as modified by Jesus, is the secret to personal transformation that will lead to church transformation that will result in cultural transformation."[46] Hull posits that the five main ingredients in Jesus's model for discipleship are (1) a disciple submits to a leader who teaches him to follow Jesus, (2) a disciple learns from Jesus's words, (3) a disciple learns Jesus's way of doing ministry, (4) a disciple imitates Jesus's life and character, and (5) a disciple finds and teaches other disciples to follow Jesus.[47]

Five Distinct Steps

James Lilly identifies five distinct steps that appear after studying Jesus's disciple-making process: (1) Jesus modeled being a disciple of His Father, (2) Jesus discipled a group of people at different intensities (as one of a multitude, as part of the Twelve, and as the three), (3) Jesus sent out the Twelve to the lost sheep of the house of Israel, (4) Jesus sent out seventy-two disciples, possibly produced by the Twelve, to the surrounding non-kosher Jews, Samaritans, and Gentiles (Luke 10:1-11), and (5) Jesus sent out the disciples to the ends of the earth once the Holy Spirit empowered them.[48]

Matthew 4:18-22

Matthew notes in this passage that Jesus's first recorded action "is to gather a group of followers, who will commit themselves to a total change of lifestyle which involves them in joining Jesus as his essential support group for the whole period of his public ministry."[49] This is significant in understanding the call Jesus made to His followers to become disciples. In calling the disciples, Jesus primarily focused on teaching them to follow and learn from Him. The disciples were mainly learners who "were expected to grow in their knowledge and understanding of God and his kingdom."[50] Collinson further notes, "This would not just be evidenced through academic cognizance but would result in growth in their faith relationship with God, affecting their attitudes, values, qualities of character, behavior and skills for continuing the works of Jesus."[51] Their growth as learners would take them beyond gaining intelligence and into an actual relationship with Jesus.

Follow Me…

Blomberg mentions that the phrase "follow me" in verse 19 literally means "come after me."[52] Culturally, it was common for learners to seek out a teacher or rabbi to become their master. In this case, it was the master, Jesus, who sought them out.[53] He not only sought them out, He "[created] his own group of disciples by calling individuals to follow him. He also [called] disciples that [did] not seem to qualify for the task."[54] The twelve were called from different backgrounds in life and were invited into a special learner-teacher relationship.[55]

Jesus issued a call to His first disciples, Peter and Andrew, and then to James and John. This call, to follow Him, "serves as a model of the nature of true discipleship generally."[56] These first disciples were not highly educated, influential, wealthy, or of high social status. They were ordinary, simple, working men with no significant background.[57] These fishermen were summoned to give up their old occupation for a new one. Bill Hull notes, "Jesus' calling of the first disciples was completely unambiguous. 'Follow me,' he said to Peter, James, John, Andrew and Matthew, and they dropped everything and followed him. They were not confused about what Jesus was asking."[58] The clear call urged on the disciples to follow Jesus and leave behind everything else.

And I will make you…

After Jesus invited the disciples to follow Him, He revealed His intentions. He asked these "fishermen to come with Him as His followers, but He also told them that He was going to change them. He said, I will make you into something."[59] Their lives would drastically change as they followed Him. He was going to teach them, train them, "and empower them to be like Himself. Jesus was going to address their beliefs, their attitudes, and actions as He shaped them into messengers who would deliver the good news to the world."[60] Nothing about their lives would be the same. Transformation was the goal.

Jesus declared that "a disciple is not above his teacher, nor a servant above his master. It is enough for the disciple to be like his teacher, and the servant like his master" (Matt 10:24-25a). In his explanation, Wilkins notes that "Becoming like Jesus includes going out with the same message, ministry, and compassion; practicing the same religious and social traditions; belonging to the same family of obedience; exercising the same servanthood; and experiencing the same suffering."[61] Discipleship has Jesus as the standard. Onyinah further explains that "Disciples are identified with the person of Jesus Christ. Their focus is to be like Christ. … The disciple follows the footsteps of Jesus."[62] To know Jesus is to follow Him closely. Ultimately, the goal is to conform to the image of Jesus (Luke 6:40).

Fishers of men…

The first disciples had been fishers of fish. Jesus said He would make them fishers of men. Jesus connected their present occupation with their future lives as followers of Christ. Jesus related to His hearers in terms they could understand.[63] Bill Hull explains how "Jesus cleverly devised his invitation for these fishermen to help them see their role. They would now employ their skills to do the same things Jesus was doing to change the nation they lived in."[64] The immediate function of those called to be fishers of men was to accompany Jesus. William Lane points out that they were to be "witnesses to the proclamation of the nearness of the kingdom and the necessity for men to turn to God through radical repentance."[65] Jesus's artistry in connecting with the disciples is an introduction to part of the discipleship process.

Hahn explains that with Jesus's call for the disciples to become fishers of men, they "immediately [turned] their attention from the demand Jesus [made] on them to the results that God desires in the lives of others."[66] They were no longer going to live their old lives and work their old occupations. Doug Redford identifies how "Jesus was inviting them to make a complete break with everything they were accustomed to—to leave business, friends, and family and to follow him."[67] Following Jesus was going to require the disciples to count the cost of their new allegiance to Jesus.

Immediately they left their nets…

Discipling relationships in the first century were a voluntary master-disciple alliance. However, Jesus made the call to follow Him, and He chose the ones whom He would call to follow. Their response "involves recognition and belief in Jesus's identity, obedience to his summons, and counting the cost of full allegiance to him."[68] They did not hesitate. Immediately, they left behind their nets, their livelihood, their past affiliations, and their planned futures. The expression, "I will make you fishers of men," "implies that they are leaving behind everything, including livelihood and home."[69] Jesus's call demanded an immediate response, and respond they did, willingly.

They did not hesitate. Immediately, they left behind their nets, their livelihood, their past affiliations, and their planned futures.

Matthew spotlights Peter's and Andrew's decisive responses to Jesus's call, indicating their understanding of the authority of Jesus's summons. As Ulrich Luz notes, "The word 'immediately' (εὐθέως) and the abandoning of the nets, which were not even pulled up on land, show the radical obedience of the two men."[70] Matthew develops a pattern for true discipleship—immediacy. Hagner adds that this pattern includes the "leaving behind of past preoccupations and unhesitating and unconditional response of following."[71] These men, without delay, began to follow Jesus. "The verb ἀκολουθεῖν, 'to follow' is important for the stress on discipleship throughout the Gospel."[72] Their response and their desire to follow Jesus was a whole-life decision. They were abandoning all that was familiar for the sake of the call.

Summary

The focus of the Great Commission is to make disciples. The pattern that Jesus established in His time on earth was to be followed by His first disciples and all future disciples in general. This method should not be thought of as strictly a teacher-student model. The final command given to his disciples was to go and make more disciples which encompassed the dissemination of information through teaching but also—and perhaps more importantly—the observation of those teachings in attitudes, values, skills, and behaviors which are appropriate for all those who are followers of God.[73]

Jesus's teachings go beyond the expectation that a disciple will simply pass knowledge on to others and takes the follower to a relationship where the teachings become a reality in the lives and actions of the disciples.[74] Bill Hull adds that "Participation in the Great Commission doesn't require great learning or ability, but it does require regeneration—being a transformed person. Only the habitation of God in a disciple enables her to answer the call to follow Christ."[75] The transformation of the disciples compelled them to follow the command Jesus gave in the Great Commission.

Discipleship in the
Old Testament

2.

The concept of discipleship is rare in the Old Testament; however, the terminology is there. The Old Testament "often speaks of walking in the ways of another, whether for good or evil."[76] Two passages, 2 Kings 21:21 and 2 Chronicles 20:32, illustrate this point. If Israel's kings followed God, then the people of Israel walked accordingly, and if the Kings followed idols, then the people of Israel followed that way after the idols. The concept of discipleship, as seen in a community or corporate setting, can also be seen to a lesser extent in one-on-one situations. Joshua is introduced as Moses' assistant (Exod 24:13; Num 11:28; Josh 1:1) "and shows [that] this service consisted of a wide range of duties of various levels of responsibility; on the one hand Joshua accompanies and provides for Moses' needs, but on the other hand he provides leadership when Moses is absent."[77] Another rendering of discipleship is the covenant relationship between God and His people. The Old Testament set the pattern for discipleship: "God's calling for Israel to be his people."[78] This ideal relationship exists as the covenant relationship between Israel and God.

The term for *disciple* is found exclusively in the Gospels and the book of Acts. In the Old Testament, the Hebrew equivalent term *limmud* is found in "Isaiah 8:16 and less directly Isaiah 50:4 and 54:13, where the same Hebrew word is translated 'learned' and 'taught,' respectively."[79] At its base definition, a disciple is a pupil of a teacher. Ryken makes mention that the teacher-learner concept is implicit in the schools of the prophets. He includes the examples of Eli-Samuel, Elisha-Gehazi, Isaiah and his assistants, and Jeremiah-Baruch.[80] These apprenticeships were primarily for the purpose of learning from the master in order to "carry on or develop his teachings after his death as in the case of Isaiah (8:16; 50:4), and especially as in the relationship of Elisha to Elijah (1 Kings 19 - 2 Kings 13)."[81] Apprenticeship allows the teacher-learner relationship to carry out the type of discipleship that continues even after the teacher-learner relationship is done.

God's call to His people is a call to discipleship. That calling began with Abram when God said, "Go from your country and your kindred and your father's house to the land I will show you" (Gen 12:1). This established "a calling motif among the covenantal people of Israel."[82] The prophet Jeremiah proclaims the words of God, "And they shall be my people, and I will be their God" (Jer 32:38), illustrating that God's presence accompanies the call to discipleship. Isaiah portrays this accompaniment in these prophetic words from God:

> But now thus says the LORD, he who created you, O Jacob, he who formed you, O Israel: "Fear not, for I have redeemed you; I have called you by name, you are mine. When you pass through the waters, I will be with you; and through the rivers, they shall not overwhelm you; when you walk through the fire you shall not be burned, and the flame shall not consume you. For I am the LORD your God, the Holy One of Israel, your Savior (Isa 43:1-3a).

From the beginning, the people of Israel were promised a close relationship with God if they would be disciples of God.

Macelaru proposes that the prominence of the relationship between Israel and God is a type of Old Testament discipleship. In his thesis, he notes three specific aspects of this relationship: (1) the relationship's beginning at Sinai (Exod 19-24) where God choose and called Israel, (2) the formative journey summarized in Jeremiah's call to truth, justice, and uprightness (Jer 4:2), and (3) the objective of the relationship to transform Israel into a community that reflects God (Lev 26; Deut 6:4-5).[83] He concludes, therefore, that the relationship "goal of discipleship according to the model discussed here is the further generation of discipleship communities, that is, of communities that are informed by truth, that act with justice and that are characterized by uprightness."[84] The discipleship journey for Israel will result in her resembling her master.[85]

Torah

God called Israel into a relationship. He initiated the call to Abram to follow, telling Abram,

> Go from your country … to the land I will show you. And I will make you a great nation, and I will bless you and make your name great, so that you will be a blessing. I will bless those who bless you, and him who dishonors you I will curse, and in you all the families of the earth shall be blessed (Gen 12:1-3).

Abram responded and headed for the place God had promised him (v. 4). This call was later repeated to Abram's son Isaac (26:3-5) and grandson Jacob (35:9-15). Israel was called by God through Abraham, Isaac, and Jacob, to be God's people. This call began a covenantal relationship with God as the master/teacher and His people as the learner disciples. This call was further delineated with Moses when God called him to go back into Egypt and rescue God's chosen ones (Exod 4:1-17).

The relationship aspect of discipleship actually began with God and His human creation—Adam and Eve (Gen 1:26-31; 2:7)—with whom God would walk in the garden in the cool of the day (3:8a). Even though they sinned (vv. 1-7) and were sent out of the garden of Eden (v. 23), God continued the relationship with them as they populated the earth. Enoch walked with God (5:24). Noah was called by God to build the ark to rescue humanity from God's punishment for humanity's sinfulness (6:14-22). Noah also walked with God (v. 9). "Walking with God" means more than a physical walk; it implies a spiritual journey in which becoming more like God is the goal. The passage in Deuteronomy 6:4-9, which defines the discipleship aspect of Israel's relationship with God, is commonly referred to as the Shema, which means "to hear."

> Hear, O Israel: The LORD our God, the LORD is one. You shall love the LORD your God with all your heart and with all your soul and with all your might. And these words that I command you today shall be on your heart. You shall teach them diligently to your children, and shall talk of them when you sit in your house, and when you walk by the way, and when you lie down, and when you rise. You shall bind them as a sign on your hand, and they shall be as frontlets between your eyes. You shall write them on the doorposts of your house and on your gates.

Walking with God on the spiritual journey of discipleship envelops every aspect of Israel's daily life and was established from the beginning of creation through God's relationship with Adam and Eve.

In the Pentateuch, there are examples of discipleship in the human-to-human aspect. After Moses' encounter with God at the burning bush, he consulted with his father-in-law, Jethro (Exod 4:18-20.) That relationship continued as Moses led the Israelites in the wilderness. Jethro gave Moses sound advice concerning his judging of the people (18:13-27). Another example of human-to-human discipleship is found in the relationship between Moses and Joshua. Joshua was referred to as Moses' aide or assistant. Joshua served with Moses even leading in his place (Josh 17:8), and on his behalf (Num 32:28). Samra notes the similarities between discipleship styles—human-to-human and God-to-human—as "Moses commissioned Joshua in the sight of the people and gave him authority from God (Num 27:18-23)."[86] Ultimately, "Just as the LORD had commanded Moses his servant, so Moses commanded Joshua, and so Joshua did. He left nothing undone of all that the LORD had commanded Moses" (Josh 11:15). Discipleship that is relational is at the heart of the Old Testament.

Walking with God on the spiritual journey of discipleship envelops every aspect of Israel's daily life.

Historical Books

As God led His chosen people through the wilderness into the Promised Land, the concept of discipleship continued. Joshua was called by God and assumed command of God's chosen people (Josh 1:10-18). As Joshua walked in the ways of the Lord, the people followed (22:5). Following their conquest of the Promised Land and the death of Joshua, God called judges to follow Him and lead the people (Judg 2:16ff). These judges were to walk in the ways of the Lord.

> Whenever the LORD raised up judges for them, the LORD was with the judge, and he saved them from the hand of their enemies all the days of the judge. For the LORD was moved to pity by their groaning because of those who afflicted and oppressed them (Judg 2:18).

God's design for discipleship was carried forward through the judges of Israel.

The final judge called by God was Samuel. Samuel was born

to a mother whose womb had been barren. She beseeched the LORD, and He gave her a son. She promised to give him back to God, and when he was of age, she brought him to Eli, the priest, to be trained for God's service (1 Sam 2:11). The relationship between Eli and Samuel displays the concept of teacher-learner interaction. Samuel learned from Eli the ways of God.

Samuel then led the people in the ways of the Lord: "And Samuel said to all the house of Israel, 'If you are returning to the LORD with all your heart, then put away the foreign gods and the Ashtaroth from among you and direct your heart to the LORD and serve him only'" (1 Sam 7:3). After Samuel anointed the first two kings of Israel, he continued to follow God and lead others. King Saul sent messengers to take David, and when they found him, they encountered Samuel and a company of prophets with him (19:20-24). Wilkins notes, "Groups of prophets were found around Samuel. He appears to have exercised some kind of 'mentor' authority over them."[87] This relationship was a teacher-learner type of relationship but not in the traditional school setting.

Following Samuel's death, the kings of Israel were either godly or ungodly with few demonstrating anything in between. The prophet Elijah appeared on the scene and delivered the word of the Lord to King Ahab (1 Kgs 17:1ff). Elijah was a prophet who walked in the ways of the Lord and led others. Elijah confronted King Ahab and 450 prophets of Baal and the 400 prophets of Asherah (18:1ff). On Mount Carmel, he challenged the Israelites to follow God (v. 21). God displayed His greatness and power through Elijah to the people of Israel. As a result, the people routed and killed the false prophets.

Elijah anointed Elisha as his successor (1 Kgs 19:16-17) by casting his cloak on him (v. 19). Stephen Szikszai notes, "This act represented a real transfer of the prophetic power to Elisha, so he followed his new master."[88] This same motif occurs in the scene when Elijah is transported in a whirlwind to heaven. Elisha took the cloak that fell from Elijah (2 Kgs 2:11-12) and so moved from being disciple to prophet.[89]

Elisha had a servant named Gehazi who followed him in his ministry as a prophet (2 Kgs 4:12). Gehazi was entrusted with Elisha's life-giving staff that was laid on the face of the dead child (v. 31). Unfortunately, he was unsuccessful, and Elisha himself revived the child (v. 32-37). Though Elisha walked in the ways of the Lord, Gehazi was prone to rudeness (v. 27) and greed (5:19-27). Elisha denounced Gehazi's greed toward Naaman and passed on the leprosy to Gehazi (vv. 20-27). Later, Gehazi appeared before King Joram and recounted the deeds of Elisha (8:1-6), thus carrying on the teacher-learner discipleship tradition.

Wisdom Books

The wisdom books contain the concept of discipleship in the form of wise sayings which help disciples walk in the ways of the Lord. There are not many examples of human-to-human discipleship; however, there are many sayings that are passed on from one follower of God to another. In Proverbs 1-9, for example, David shares with his son Solomon instructions for walking with God. He instructs on knowledge: "The fear of the Lord is the beginning of knowledge; fools despise wisdom and instruction" (Prov 1:7). He instructs Solomon on sin: "My son, if sinners entice you, do not consent" (v. 10). He instructs on wisdom: "My son, if you receive my words and treasure up my commandments with you, making your ear attentive to wisdom and inclining your heart to understanding … then you will understand the fear of the LORD and find the knowledge of God" (2:1-2, 5). He instructs on the ways of wisdom and the ways of folly (Prov 9). And he instructs on matters of the heart: "Trust in the LORD with all your heart, and do not lean on your own understanding. In all your ways acknowledge him, and he will make your paths straight" (3:5-6). Instruction in wisdom and knowledge is an important part of a growing disciple.

The book of Job describes the detailed story of the life of a man named Job. The relationship between Job and God is developed along with his relationship with his wife and his friends. Clearly, his relationship with God is the baseline for Job's growing understanding of what it means to walk in the ways of the Lord. Job confesses, "I know that you can do all things, and that no purpose of yours can be thwarted" (Job 42:2). Whether through difficult times or times of great blessing, Job found walking in the ways of the Lord to be fulfilling.

Clearly, Job's relationship with God is the baseline for his growing understanding of what it means to walk in the ways of the Lord.

Ecclesiastes is written as a book of instruction from a teacher.[90] The life-lessons the teacher provides include the general futility of life (Eccl 1), the meaningless of a self-centered life (Eccl 1-2), life's experiences (3-11), and the concluding challenges (11:7-12:14). The end of the matter, the teacher concludes, is to "Fear God and keep his commandments, for this is the whole duty of man" (12:13). The teacher instructs the student to commit to God.

Psalm 119 serves as a model and pattern for relationship with God that both grows in dependence upon God and desire for God's ways. Those who walk in God's ways are blameless (119:1). They store God's Word in their hearts so they might not sin against him (v. 11). They desire to be taught the ways of the Lord (v. 33) and long for his precepts (v. 40). They understand that God is near, and his commandments are true (v. 151). Ultimately, they long for his salvation (v. 176).

Prophets

The concept of discipleship in the writings of the prophets is described in terms of the covenant with God and Israel. The relationship between Israel and their God is laid bare as God speaks to His people through the words and actions of the prophets. Jeremiah describes the dynamics of this relationship by declaring, "And if you swear, 'As the LORD lives,' in truth, in justice, and in righteousness, then nations shall bless themselves in him, and in him shall they glory" (Jer 4:2). Isaiah describes Israel's ultimate realization of that active relationship with God by pointing out,

> And though the Lord give you the bread of adversity and the water of affliction, yet your Teacher will not hide himself anymore, but your eyes shall see your Teacher. And your ears shall hear a word behind you, saying, 'This is the way, walk in it,' when you turn to the right or when you turn to the left (Isa 30:20-21).

Micah reiterates this covenantal relationship: "He has told you, O man, what is good; and what does the LORD require of you but to do justice, and to love kindness, and to walk humbly with your God" (Mic 6:8). Ultimately, the covenant relationship requires actions as well as words.

A teacher-student relationship between Jeremiah and Baruch illustrates the discipleship concept of human-to-human mentoring. Baruch is described as an amanuensis (Jer 36:4), meaning he acted as Jeremiah's representative concerning a written document (32:12-15), and was taken, along with Jeremiah, into captivity in Egypt (43:6).[91] Baruch received a word from the Lord in the same manner that Jeremiah did. Jeremiah ultimately wrote words of encouragement to Baruch concerning his life and the destruction of Jerusalem (45:1-5). The student's growth can be seen in the life of Baruch.

Summary

God called Israel into a special relationship. This relationship guaranteed His presence in their lives and circumstances. Wilkins posits that Old Testament discipleship relationships can be observed on three levels: "(1) on a national level, in the covenant relationship of Israel and God; (2) on the individual to God level, in the relationship of certain individuals who followed God; and (3) on the human relationship level, in relationships found within the national life."[92] Within these three levels, in the Old Testament, from the Torah through the Prophets, discipleship is on display. Ultimately, the Old Testament patterns of discipleship find their fulfillment in the coming of the Messiah, Jesus, and His call for disciples to follow Him.

3. Discipleship in the New Testament

The concept of discipleship in the New Testament "is firmly rooted in the Old Testament, in the idea of the forming and calling of Israel out of the nations to be God's peculiar treasure and to bear testimony to his name among the nations."[93] Just as God called Abram, Jesus called the Twelve to leave their former lives and follow Him. Jesus's call was a restating of the call God offered to Israel centuries earlier. As God directed Abram to leave his current life and go to the country of the promise (Gen 12:1), Jesus reiterated this challenge in Mark 8:34-35: "If anyone would come after me, let him deny himself and take up his cross and follow me. For whoever would save his life would lose it, but whoever loses his life for my sake, and the gospel's will save it."[94]

The disciples walked with Jesus in His earthly ministry, "and the passion of their ministry was to bring Jesus alive in the hearts and lives of those around them."[95] This is the meaning of discipleship. The things they were taught they began to put into practice after Jesus's ascension to heaven. Discipleship during the early ministry years of Jesus "must be adjusted in the age of the early church, and today, to having an ascended Master who is now at the right hand of the Father."[96] The form of discipleship that Jesus developed was distinctive "and by the time he issued the Great Commission to 'make disciples' of all nations, his followers knew what his kind of disciple would look like, and what the life of discipleship to the ascended Jesus would look like."[97] They learned from the teacher and put all that knowledge into practice after His ascension.

Robert Webber posits that there are three aspects of discipleship that stand out in the early Christian era: believing, belonging, and behaving.[98] To be a disciple of Jesus, "one must believe what the Bible teaches about him (John 20:31). A disciple must belong to a community of believers (Acts 2:42-47). A disciple is also called to a new life of ethical behavior (Rom 12:2)."[99] The disciples understood that discipleship is part of an ongoing process. Discipleship is not something that must be achieved at a certain level of maturity. Gibbs explains the realization of the disciples "that an essential ingredient of discipleship is the making of other disciples."[100] Spiritual maturity is a result of a disciple being a growing believer.

> *There are three aspects of discipleship that stand out in the early Christian era: believing, belonging, and behaving.*
> —Robert Webber

The common use of the term *disciple* had at its core understanding the idea of being a learner or follower. The word disciple is used 230 times in the Gospels and another twenty-eight times in Acts. Conversely, the term *Christian* appears in the New Testament only three times and *believer* appears nine times.[101] Disciple is "the primary term used in the Gospels to refer to Jesus' followers and is a common referent for those known in the early church as believers, Christians, brothers/sisters, those of the way, or saints."[102] Those who followed Jesus after His ascension were also called disciples as they "regarded their relationship to the risen Lord Jesus in some way similar to the relationship of the first disciples to the earthly 'rabbi' Jesus."[103]

The use of the term *disciple* in the Gospels and Acts begins to transition to other terminology in later books. These other terms were more appropriate to the community of believers after Jesus's resurrection. In the book of Acts, although disciple was still an important term, "a transition to other terms began to occur. One description that naturally expressed the new relationship with the risen Lord was 'believers' (Acts 5:14, 10:45)."[104] Therefore, though the writers of the New Testament use differing terminology to describe a follower of Jesus, at the heart, all the terms trace back to disciple and its meaning.

Table 1: Terms equivalent to *disciple* in the Gospels, transitioning through Acts and the Epistles/Revelation[105]

Gospels	Acts	Epistles
disciple = believers	disciple = believers	believers
disciple = brothers/sisters	disciple = brothers/sisters	brothers/sisters
disciple = servants	disciple = servants	servants
disciple = church	disciple = church	church

Table 2: Terms equivalent to disciple in the book of Acts, transitioning through the Epistles/Revelation

Gospels	Acts	Epistles
Disciple	disciple = saint	saint
Disciple	disciple = Christians	Christians

Table 3: Related teachings and metaphors of the discipleship life found in the Gospels, Acts, and Epistles/Revelation

Teachings	**Metaphors**
Following Jesus	Walking
Bearing the Cross	Shepherd and Sheep
Marks of Discipleship	Branches
Light of the World	Imitation
Prayer	
Pattern of Righteousness	

Gospels and Acts

Jesus's discipleship methods are made clear in the four Gospels and the book of Acts. In the Gospels, Jesus called His disciples "to abandon their previous lifestyle, denying personal ambition, comfort and safety and, as his followers, to embark on a radically different life within the family of God."[106] This choice is never pictured as being easy, "but it is essential for those who claim to be people of God."[107] The more time the disciples spent with Jesus, the more they were identified with Him. Shirley lists three qualifications for true disciples: "(1) Belief in Jesus as messiah (John 2:11; 6:68-69); (2) Commitment to identity with him through baptism; (3) Obedience to his teaching and submission to his Lordship (Matt 19:23-30; Luke 14:25-33)."[108]

In Matthew's tome, Jesus's initial call to follow and the disciple's response was the beginning of the disciple's voluntary commitment to learning from the teacher (Matt 4:18-22; 9:9-13; 10:1-4). This followed the traditional teacher-learner model of discipleship except for the teacher called the students. The teacher then instructed the students in a formal setting in the Sermon on the Mount (Matt 5-7). After the Sermon on the Mount, the practical side of the formal instruction began and continued until the end of Matthew's Gospel.

Jesus sent the twelve disciples out into the towns to the lost sheep of the house of Israel (Matt 10:5-15). He also, at various times, took three of the twelve for more personal training such as during His transfiguration (17:1-13) and at the garden of Gethsemane (26:36-46). After His death and resurrection (27:32-28:10), Jesus gathered His disciples and gave them the Great Commission (28:18-20). From Matthew's Gospel, "it can be seen that the distinctive character of discipleship for Matthew is determined by (1) the person to whom disciples give their allegiance and (2) the nature of the relationship established between disciples and teachers."[109] Jesus defines the nature of the discipleship relationship in a different light.

David Putman believes that the foundational passage introducing what it means to be a follower of Jesus is Mark 3:13-15: "And he went up on the mountain and called those whom he desired, and they came to him. And he appointed twelve (whom he named apostles) so that they might be with him and he might send them out to preach and have authority to cast out demons."[110] Putnam adds that Jesus chose twelve men "who would help him accomplish His work and in whom He would invest His life."[111] Mark closes his Gospel with the account of Jesus appearing to Mary Magdalene (Mark 16:9-11) and two other disciples walking on the road (vv. 12-13). Afterward, He called His disciples together and told them to "Go into all the world and proclaim the gospel to the whole creation" (v. 15).

Luke's Gospel details the beginning of Jesus' ministry (Luke 4:31-34). Jesus explains the cost of following Him (9:23-25):

> If anyone would come after me, let him deny himself and take up his cross daily and follow me. For whoever would save his life will lose it, but whoever loses his life for my

sake will save it. For what does it profit a man if he gains the whole world and loses or forfeits himself?

Jesus also spoke to the great crowds who accompanied Him about the cost of following Him (14:25-33). After Jesus's death and resurrection, Luke notes that Jesus appeared to two disciples on the road to Emmaus (24:13-35) and then to His disciples (vv. 36-49) before His ascension (vv. 50-53). Luke details throughout his account that following Jesus would be costly but valuable.

John's Gospel tells the story of John the Baptist who testified and baptized Jesus (John 1:19-34). Jesus then called His first disciples (vv. 35-51). He told them to bear fruit and prove thus they were His disciples (15:8). Jesus promised and did indeed send a Helper (16:5-15) to assist in the continuation of His ministry after His ascension.

The transition in discipleship from the Gospels—in which Jesus called, trained, sent, and gave the Holy Spirit—to Acts is distinct and unique. The teacher ascended to the right hand of God and left His personally trained disciples to carry on His disciple-making model. Jesus did not "expect His followers to accomplish this seemingly overwhelming task without His assistance. They were commissioned to go under His authority (Matt 28:18) and in the power of the Holy Spirit (Acts 1:8)."[112] Jesus promised them they would receive this power "when the Holy Spirit has come upon you, and you will be my witnesses in Jerusalem and in all Judea and Samaria, and to the end of the earth" (Acts 1:8). Just as in the words of the Great Commission, Jesus promised to be with His disciples always, this time through the power of the Holy Spirit.

The signs of discipleship in the Early Church were evident in Acts 2:42-47. The followers of Christ "devoted themselves to the apostles' teaching and the fellowship, to the breaking of bread and the prayer" (v. 42). The behavior which the Early Church displayed was simple yet profound. Rohde notes, "The Spirit of

Christ lived in every believer in an abiding relationship. He spoke to them, and they obeyed him because he was their Lord. This loving obedience was lived out in every aspect of life both individually and in loving community."[113] Bill Hull points out that the phrase "each day" ("day by day," ESV) is used twice in this passage. He posits that this repetitious phrase is a good thing because it shows that these practices

Daily living out the aspects of New Testament discipleship is what the Early Church did.

here were routine.[114] He continues, "When activities are routine, they form our habits and become embedded practices of a community, forming the community's culture and the worldview."[115] Daily living out the aspects of New Testament discipleship is what the Early Church did.

Acts 2:42-47 details five priorities practiced by the Early Church that developed the Church into a reproducing Church: (1) a commitment to Scripture (v. 42); (2) a commitment to one another (vv. 42, 44, 46); (3) a commitment to prayer (v. 42); (4) a commitment to praise and worship (vv. 43, 47); and (5) a commitment to outreach (vv. 45-47). These priorities are not listed here as one-time occurrences but were done continually. Newman posits that the Greek text of this verse literally means "they were devoting themselves (italics added) to the apostles' teachings and to the fellowship, to the breaking of bread and to prayers."[116] Discipleship is an ongoing, continuous growing process.

One of the best examples of disciple-making in the New Testament (apart from Jesus and His disciples), belongs to Barnabas. Barnabas was sent to Antioch by the church in Jerusalem to evaluate the report from the church there (Acts 11:19-24). Barnabas then left Antioch and headed to Tarsus to look for Saul. When he found Saul, he brought him to Antioch, and for one year, they met with the church and taught the people (v. 26). Barnabas was an encourager, and because of his faith, Saul, later Paul, became a powerful voice in the Church.

Barnabas and Paul travelled and proclaimed the good news in many regions. In Derbe, "When they preached the gospel to

One of the best examples of disciple-making in the New Testament (apart from Jesus and His disciples), belongs to Barnabas.

that city and had made many disciples, they returned to Lystra and to Iconium and to Antioch" (Acts 14:21). Kvalbein explains that "the verb 'make disciples,' is seldom used in the New Testament and has different meanings. The use of this verb in Acts 14:21 (*matheteuo*) is most close to the use in the great commission."[117] Paul and Barnabas both preached and made disciples.

Paul's Writings

Paul was discipled by Barnabas, but it was his experience with the risen Christ on the road to Damascus that first changed his life (Acts 9:1-19). Paul then lived the rest of his life in pursuit of Jesus, pouring himself out like a drink offering (Phil 2:17). Charles Davis notes how, for all disciples, "This lifelong process of learning to know Jesus is a journey of becoming more and more like him. No one crossed the finish line in this life. Even Paul continued to strain toward the goal."[118] The discipling process was lifelong, even for Paul.

Paul understood that his life belonged to Jesus (Phil 1:21); therefore, he gave himself fully to proclaiming Christ and Christ crucified (1 Cor 2:2). Paul understood the power of transformation (2 Cor 3:18) and the need to be transformed by the renewing of the mind (Rom 12:2). In Galatians 4:19-20, Paul writes: "My little children, for whom I am again in the anguish of childbirth until Christ is formed in you! I wish I could be present with you now." Shirley notes about the verb "formed" in verse 19 that "Another common word derived from the suffix 'scipe' is 'shape,' which means to create or form."[119] In these verses, Paul shared his longing to see "spiritual formation occur in the lives of the Galatian disciples—that their discipleship would produce changed lives and provide evidence that transformation was occurring."[120] Ultimately, discipleship is being formed and transformed by Jesus.

Paul's life was lived for Jesus, and the disciple-making model Jesus exemplified was also exemplified in Paul. In 2 Timothy 2:2 Paul writes, "And what you have heard from me in the presence of many witnesses entrust to faithful men who will be able to teach others also.[121] Paul passed down the faith to others and encouraged them to do the same.

General Epistles

The writers of the New Testament books known as the General Epistles continued the discipleship model that Jesus commanded in the Great Commission. Wilkins identifies how "Peter knows well what discipleship to Jesus entailed, and guides the early church into discipleship to Jesus in the post-resurrection age."[122] Peter himself writes about following the discipleship model demonstrated by Jesus: "For to this you have been called, because Christ also suffered for you, leaving you an example, so that you might follow in his steps" (1 Pet 2:21). Following Jesus's example means walking in His ways.

Other writers encouraged followers of Jesus in their walk with God. James writes, "And let steadfastness have its full effect, that you may be perfect and complete, lacking in nothing" (Jas 1:4). The author of Hebrews wanted believers to grow. He writes, "For though by this time you ought to be teachers, you need someone to teach you again the basic principles of the oracles of God" (Heb 5:12). John encouraged the believers to love one another (1 John 3:11), and he further writes, "By this we know love, that he laid down his life for us, and we ought to lay down our lives for the brothers" (v. 16). In daily living, disciples are to encourage each other and love as Jesus loved them.

Figure 1. Paul's Discipleship[123]

Summary

The disciple-making model Jesus lived was one that the disciples practiced following His ascension. They heeded the commands of the Great Commission as they went into all the world making disciples, baptizing, and teaching new disciples to obey all Jesus commanded. The threads of discipleship are evident from Matthew to Revelation.

Conclusion to Part One

Wilkins posits that there are five main characteristics of disciples:

1. disciples are learners,

2. disciples are committed believers,

3. disciples are ministers,

4. disciples are converts, and

5. disciples are converts who are in the process of discipleship.[124]

Disciples are those who respond to the Great Commission's call to make disciples in all nations. They are to live as Jesus lived and follow His example as a disciple-maker. They are to follow Christ and forsake their old ways as they journey in "the adventure of being mere disciples."[125]

PART TWO

"No one accidentally creates disciples. Discipleship is an intentional pursuit." —Mike Breen[126]

Jesus called the twelve disciples to leave their already established lives and follow Him. The new life that He promised was one of relationship and transformation. They would become disciple-makers just like Him. He encouraged and walked alongside them as He prepared them for their new occupation. Making disciples is the essence of discipleship. The command to make disciples is the same today as it was to the first disciples. Learning to walk in the ways of Jesus—and learning to walk alongside other disciples as they grow and mature—builds on the foundational call to make disciples.

This part of the book discusses the heart of discipleship—the command to make disciples—as well as how disciple-making takes place in church practice. Finally, I consider the nature of whole-life disciple-making in terms of the two dimensions of spiritual formation and personal wholeness.

4.

The Heart of
Discipleship

The command to make disciples is at the heart of discipleship. When Jesus gave the Great Commission in Matthew 28:16-20 to His disciples, He identified what should be the crux of their focus. Beverly Vos summarizes that "being disciples and making disciples is the core business of Christian ministry."[127] Opoku Onyinah confirms that discipleship "is not just following [Jesus'] principles, ideas, or philosophy. It is not primarily conceptual, but it is personal. The disciple aims at Christlikeness."[128] Obeying the command to make disciples should be the focus of the Church and Christ's disciples. Making disciples and growing as disciples are the goals.

Growth as a follower of Jesus is not linear. Robert Logan and Charles Ridley address this noting that it "is not a straight-arrow shot from A to Z. Instead, they *(disciples)* take steps forward, along with missteps, steps back, lapses, and sometimes relapses— metaphorically falling off the wagon."[129] Each disciple's growth rate is different in both timing and kind. This requires disciple-makers to "have patience with the process of growth and respect for individual differences."[130] This individualization of development is part of the uniqueness of each disciple.

The goal of a disciple is to be like Jesus. This is an on-going process that involves both intellectual learning and hands-on experience. Developing a discipling culture within the church is vital to the maturing of disciples. Mike Breen posits that to build a discipling culture, three things are necessary: (1) a discipleship vehicle, (2) access to each other's lives, and (3) a discipling language.[131] These three components were part of Jesus's discipling pattern: (1) He invested in a small number of people, (2) He built relationships with each follower, and (3) He founded and continues to build His Church.

The goal of a disciple is to be like Jesus.

A disciple is one who is growing to be like Jesus and conforming to His image. Russell Huizing states that Jesus took a group of untrained individuals, "and within a short period of time had qualified them to lead his mission to change the world—which they promptly began to do."[132] In this process, Huizing continues, "theologians typically refer to his method of doing this as discipleship."[133] Jesus's discipleship model was more than the traditional teacher-student model. Jesus's model encompassed more than information; it included the observation of Jesus's life and the making of new disciples. Michael Wilkins describes discipleship as

> living a fully human life in this world in union with Jesus Christ, growing in conformity to his image as the Spirit transforms us from the inside-out, nurtured within a community of disciples who are engaged in that lifelong process, and helping others to know and become like him.[134]

Disciples making disciples is the basis of discipleship.[135]

In writing about the modern Church losing sight of the biblical term *disciple*, Edward Gross laments that "Discipleship not done became discipleship lost."[136] He notes that it is not lack of biblical knowledge that has caused this, but it is that "the biblical concept of discipleship has been forgotten by many Christians."[137] Discipleship, in many ways, has become a program rather than an activity to be done by the disciples. James wrote for believers to

> But be doers of the word, and not hearers only, deceiving yourselves. For if anyone is a hearer of the word and not a doer, he is like a man who looks intently at his natural face in a mirror. For he looks at himself and goes away and at once forgets what he was like. But the one who looks into the perfect law, the law of liberty, and perseveres, being no hearer who forgets but a doer who acts, he will be blessed in his doing (1:22-25).

Both discipleship and the biblical meaning of disciple need to be recovered.

The result of the loss of discipleship in the church is that "Not-yet-believers and new believers have no examples to follow and no mature believers assisting them in their discipleship."[138] The relationships vital to discipleship are missing. Bill Hull adds that "enough of the church has accepted a nondiscipleship Christianity to render it ineffective at its primary task—the transformation of individuals and communities into the image of Christ."[139] For the "church to be deficient in discipleship is to be deficient in its fundamental reason for existence. If any organization is careless in its core reason for existence, it doesn't matter if the organization excels at other things."[140] The primary task often becomes a secondary task or even an afterthought.

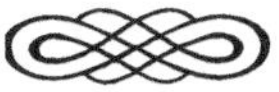

"Effective discipleship builds the church, not the other way around. We need to understand the church as the effect of discipleship and not the cause."
—Mike Breen

Competent discipleship is critical for the growth of the church. Unfortunately, many believers have the purpose of discipleship twisted. Breen posits that "Effective discipleship builds the church, not the other way around. We need to understand the church as the effect of discipleship and not the cause."[141] The modern Church places a high emphasis on increasing membership to the church to the omission of actually making disciples. Breen continues, noting, "If you set out to build the church, there is no guarantee you will make disciples. It is far more likely that you will create consumers who depend on the spiritual services that religious professionals provide."[142] In making disciples through discipleship, the church is naturally built.

Paul Tanner uses the phrase "comfortable Christianity" in describing non-discipleship churches. He writes that it "is the siren seductively luring us to crash on the rocks of personal ruin."[143] Comfortable Christianity causes believers to be more interested in the things of this world rather than the life God requires and desires for His followers. He concludes that "if we truly value our lives, we would be concerned for what we can have to gain for all eternity, not merely for what we can have in this world."[144] Bobby Harrington and Josh Patrick point out these differences in focus as outlined in Table 4.

Table 4: Biblical Faith[145]

Cultural Christianity	**Biblical Faith**
I like the things of Jesus being part of my life.	Jesus is at the center of my life.
I have a life and Jesus is in parts of it.	I form my life around Jesus.
I believe that Jesus was a good man/teacher.	I believe Jesus is Savior and Lord.

I was christened/made a one-time decision.	I trust and follow Jesus daily.
I pray to God when I need help.	I pray to God and seek His guidance daily.
God will save me; I am a good person.	God will save me; I have faith in Jesus.
God will forgive my sins because I am human.	God will forgive my sins because of Jesus.

For the disciple, a life that is Christ-centered is one that leaves the comfortable behind and is lived out with biblical faith.

5. *Disciple-Making in* Church Practice

Transformational/Relational

Discipleship in daily practice can be spoken of as transformational, relationship-centered, community-involved, and in a broader sense, forming the local church.[146] Discipleship should be action-oriented and intentional. However, not all believers share this view of discipleship. Jim Putman and Bobby Harrington write that

> When you ask most evangelicals what their job as a believer is, they may tell you that they are to share Christ, but how many actually do? At worst, they follow the rule that you don't talk about politics and religion, and they will die without ever seeing anyone come to faith. At best, they may invite people to church, but they think making disciples is not their job; it's the pastor's job.[147]

The command to make disciples becomes an esprit d'escalier (reply thought of too late) at best or omitted at worse. Jesus's command "represents the purposes of ministry, not an afterthought. And discipleship doesn't happen by sitting in a spiritual greenhouse, but by design, effort, and perseverance on an individual level."[148] The discipleship command is a call to action.

Discipleship results in transformation. Biblical transformation means to be changed to the image of Christ. Romans 12:1-2 illustrates this change:

> I appeal to you therefore, brothers, by the mercies of God, to present your bodies as a living sacrifice, holy and acceptable to God, which is your spiritual worship. Do not be conformed to this world, but be transformed by the renewal of your mind, that by testing you may discern what is the will of God, what is good and acceptable and perfect.

Bennett adds that the term transformed "comes from the Greek word morpho, which influenced the English word 'metamorphosis' and means to 'change into another form.'"[149] Transformation and the producing of transformed lives moves the church in the direction of its intended mission.[150] Onyinah writes that "the strength and influence of the church is wholly dependent upon its commitment to true discipleship; producing transformed lives, and seeing those lives reproduced in others."[151] Fulfilling the Great Commission is accomplished through lives transformed through discipleship.

The goal for the believer is "not only to learn how to live like Christ, but to actually live like Christ. This involves nothing less than radical life change."[152] A transformed life is developed in Christ-centered discipleship. It can be noted that "Discipleship apart from Jesus is nontransformational. It may bring changes, but it essentially leaves you in the same spiritual state as it found you."[153] If discipleship is not transformational, then it is not biblical

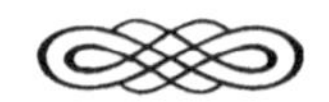

A transformed life is developed in Christ-centered discipleship.

discipleship. Geiger, Kelley, and Nation add that "we can confidently assert that most churches are deficient in discipleship. This is a scathing claim as our entire mission as believers and churches is to 'make disciples.'"[154] The Church, in general, needs a re-focus toward biblical discipleship.

Greg Ogden asserts that there are necessary elements for transformation and growth in maturity in Christ.[155] First is multiplication or reproduction. This is "empowering those who are discipled to disciple others."[156] Second is intimate relationships. These relationships develop "deep trust as the soil for life [changes]."[157] The third element is accountability or "lovingly speaking truth into another's life."[158] Fourth is the incorporation of the biblical message. This requires "covering the themes of Scripture sequentially to create a holistic picture of the Christian life."[159] And the fifth element is the spiritual disciplines. This is "practicing the habits that lead to intimacy with Christ and service to others."[160] These five elements that lead to growth and transformation are fully developed in a discipleship setting.

The transformation that takes place begins not "with something we do. It begins with something Christ did."[161] The continuing transformation is a work of the Holy Spirit and relationships that are built in the discipleship area. Onyinah adds that "Although Christ-likeness is the ultimate goal of the disciple, God uses human agents in this transformational work."[162] Relationships are vital to disciple-making. Jesus spent the better part of three years in relationship building with His disciples. His pattern is meant to be followed in developing disciples today. "The human agent must have already become a disciple, since whether for good or for bad, the disciple will become like the teacher. Thus, it is essential for every believer discipling another to exhibit the traits of Jesus."[163] This is the backbone of disciple-making.

Discipleship is relational. The author of Hebrews reminds

readers of this:

> Let us hold fast the confession of our hope without wavering, for he who promised is faithful. And let us consider how to stir up one another to love and good works, not neglecting to meet together, as is the habit of some, but encouraging one another, and all the more as you see the Day drawing near (Heb 10:23-25).

The author emphasizes the necessity of relationships between believers who meet together. In these relationships, believers are encouraging one another to good works and love. The relationships begin with the hope that is found in Christ. Julia Duin concludes that "Christianity is by nature relational, including the provision that one is saved from eternal death by believing on actions performed by someone else, namely, God incarnate."[164] This is the root of discipleship. This relationship with Jesus "transforms our hearts, minds, and behaviors to be what Jesus teaches and demands they should be."[165] The relationship with Christ is then lived out in relationships with other believers and unbelievers. It is "through the disciples' relationships with one another—especially between mature believers—[that] there is personal and collective growth. Disciple-making relationships positively impact all walks of life and all relationships in family, community, business, and government."[166] Disciple-making affects all areas of life and is built upon the establishment of relationships

Onyinah posits that "the key to disciple-making is life-on-life relationships."[167] Relationships are grounded in Christ and provide "context for practical application" for the believer and the new believer.[168] The relationships between believers are necessary for growth; however, discipleship involves more than Sunday morning worship, preaching, listening, or attending a class. True discipleship "integrates intimate, accountable relationships that are rooted in the Word of God, which cultivates enduring, fruitful lives."[169] The dynamics of relationships lead to maturity and growth.[170]

In their work on discipleship, Robert Logan and Charles Ridley examine the fact that not every relationship is a discipling relationship.[171] They write that discipling relationships are identified by "the context in which disciples are made and developed. It is specifically geared toward growth and developing the kind of people Jesus talked about in the Great Commission— disciples who make disciples who make disciples."[172] It is with this purpose that they posit discipling relationships have four defining features. First, such relationships are intentional. "A discipling relationship [is one] with a purpose. It's not just casual—it's a relationship headed toward a goal. It's on purpose, intentional."[173] Second, discipling relationships are developmental. "A good discipling relationship … takes people wherever they are and helps them move one step further."[174] Third, these kinds of relationships are supportive. "We're not just engaging in strategic planning; we're coming alongside like Barnabas and cheering people on."[175] And, finally, discipling relationships are focused. "There is clarity about where you're trying to go and what you're trying to produce."[176] Logan and Ridley conclude that a discipling relationship has clear, practical goals that distinguish it from other types of relationships.[177]

Relationships developed through the discipleship aspect lead to community. The journey "of disciple-making and Christian formation is clearly ordered around the cycle of believing, behaving, and belonging and is accomplished in the context of the worshipping community."[178] In the life of the believer, community is vital. In the Christian community, the disciple's identity is nourished. In this, "Each individual enjoys a personal relationship with Christ that facilitates transformation into his image, but that personal relationship must be nurtured within two primary communities of faith—the spiritual family and the biological family."[179] Though discipleship is personal, it is collaborative in character.[180]

This collaboration is something special about Christian communities. A collaborative "community is a group of people who gather regularly. … These are the people we gather together with to live out the one-anothers of Scriptures toward the end of all of us becoming better disciples."[181] Ron Bennett describes this as a spiritual construction company. At its core mission is the building of strong communities. "By building sound homes— not entertainment centers, hospitals, theological universities, warehouses, shopping malls, community centers, or political action organizations. These homes represent the transformation of individual lives."[182] He concludes that churches would do well to hang up an "under construction" sign.[183]

John O'Grady asserts that one cannot separate Jesus and the church. Jesus gathered a community around himself. "We can understand the church as a continuation of this community."[184] This is disclosed when what Jesus taught and what He did is viewed via His ministry. O'Grady adds that "No one can ever separate Jesus from the church and vice versa. Nor can anyone separate Jesus and the church from the testimony that forms the New Testament."[185] When a community of believers gathers for worship, they gather in Jesus's name. This is the essence of the community gathering as a local church.

The use of the term *disciples* "reminds us that the church from the beginning was the 'school' of Jesus. Therefore, the teaching function must be very important in the church. But the only real teacher is Jesus himself. The church is basically a fellowship of his students."[186] A disciple is a learner who learns from the teacher. Aubrey Malphurs concurs:

> Jesus was clear about his intentions for his church. It wasn't just to teach or preach the Word, as important as that is. Nor was it evangelism alone, although this is emphasized as

much as teaching. He expects his entire church (not simply a few passionate disciple makers) to move people along a maturity or disciple—making continuum from prebirth (unbelief) to the new birth (belief) and then to maturity.[187]

Disciple-making remains the primary task for the church. In making disciples, the church "ensures that the gospel is embedded deeply in the lives of mature believers who serve as links to the future."[188] The church needs to make disciples by following in the footsteps of Jesus and His disciple-making model.

The pattern that Jesus modeled was to "go to where the people are—and that's outside the walls of the church. We are to meet them where they are geographically and spiritually."[189] The church cannot stay contained inside the four walls of the building. The call is to make disciples of all nations. Often the call is misinterpreted to mean joining a church or a movement. Many churches try and "have failed at Disciple-Making not only for lack of trying, but because they do not know what being a disciple of Jesus means. We don't know what a disciple is because we ourselves have not been disciples in the same sense that those who followed Jesus were disciples."[190] Following Jesus's model for disciple-making is where the church needs to return.

> *The church needs to make disciples by following in the foot-steps of Jesus and His disciple-making model.*

Intentional/Informational

Discipleship is intentional. It is done with purpose. There is nothing coincidental about making disciples. Discipleship is "not something we can accidently drift towards or into. It is something we must give our full attention to, intentionally determining to make ourselves apprentices, no matter what the cost."[191] In being intentional, disciples willingly live their lives in relationship with other believers. Disciple-making "is a relationship where we intentionally walk alongside a growing disciple or disciples in order to encourage, correct and challenge them in love to grow toward maturity."[192] Intentionality is necessary in disciple-making for spiritual growth to happen.

The modern Church's understanding of discipleship has shifted from the model of the church being a part of the community to being centered around the church building. The emphasis has become informational and educational.[193] The amount of information about spiritual things, God's Word, and traditions, has usurped the place of transformation. Bob Roberts writes that the emphasis "must shift from information to transformation."[194] Information is vital in the discipleship process,

> but it is not the most important aspect of the disciple-making process. Disciples do not just know what the Master requires in every situation regardless of the consequences. Not every situation is delineated in Scripture, but all the principles are there for disciples to apply to daily living. Understanding the principles of Scripture and knowing the mind of God are crucial in the disciple-making process.[195]

Discipleship is not only about the amount of information studied and remembered, but "about a lifestyle that is practiced. It is a lifestyle of absolute abandonment to loving God and obeying His commands."[196] Roberts concurs with this summation, declaring, "Information downloading is easy. In contrast, transformational living doesn't require huge amounts of information, but it does require the constant practice of what you know."[197] Information in and of itself is not the answer. It is in transformational living that discipleship thrives.

Teaching disciples to observe all that Jesus commanded is part of the Great Commission. Often teaching becomes the central focus. Larry Osborne states that "Jesus didn't tell us to go and make disciples of all nations, teaching them great doctrine. He told us to, 'Go and make disciples of all nations … teaching them to obey everything I have commanded you.'"[198] Discipleship is relational in nature. The contrast can be seen in the table below.

Table 5: Educational Discipleship versus Relational Discipleship[199]

EDUCATIONAL DISCIPLESHIP	INTENTIONAL RELATIONAL DISCIPLESHIP
Requires sole attention to Scripture	Requires a personal relationship pointed to Jesus
Depends on Scripture and Holy Spirit	Depends on Scripture, the Holy Spirit, and relationships
Focuses on the head	Focuses on the head, heart, and hands
Academic in nature	Teaching/modeling/ coaching in nature
Emphasizes factual knowledge	Emphasizes life application
Information focused	Transformation focused
Content based	Supportive relationship
No breaking of bread. Time involved is inconsistent and limited	Breaking of bread in homes together. Time involved is daily, personal, and extensive

Teacher has all the answers	Let's figure it out together
Large group	Small group
Building/campus	Home
General Attitude: The lesson is the agenda	General Attitude: We're doing life together
Setting is formal	Setting is casual

Churches have created and developed discipleship processes that are nothing more than information downloading, i.e., classroom teaching. Breen notes that this style involves "Hear the sermon. Join the small group. Go to the membership class. Read your Bible (hopefully you figure out how to do it). Go to class 201 or 301, and 'yes, we have a class for that.'"[200] Although there is room for classroom teaching in discipleship, it is not enough to simply gather information. There is the transformational component that requires action to go along with what is learned. It is not just about knowledge, it is

> about character, behavior, attitudes, a posture of humility, teachability—and grace for continued growth. Knowledge may be a building block, but it's not enough on its own. By itself, knowledge puffs up. The heart of discipleship displays Jesus to those around us in a way that they can see. If there's something real on the inside, it needs to be observable on the outside. Inner qualities can only be seen through behaviors.[201]

The information must work its way into the disciple and be incarnated in the disciple. If it is information, then it is "information that has worked its way into you and is now part of you."[202] Information at work in the disciple gives deeper meaning to discipleship.

Discipleship is simple terms can "be said to be the process of helping to produce Christ-like character in a believer by another person."[203] The understanding of discipleship has changed over time. It has "shifted-from an ongoing process over the course of one's life to a class you sign up for and complete."[204] Because of this change in understanding, the church has been losing its influence in communities. "Those Christ calls the churches to reach, no longer flock to our church programs or services."[205] True discipleship is relational and not program oriented.

In modern churches, "we have replaced person-centered growth with programs as the means of making disciples."[206] Ogden describes programs as "structured group methods we use to herd large groups of people through systems.[207] Program discipleship tends to encourage more individual discipleship. Solo discipleship proposes that believers only take part in "activities or spiritual exercises that I have time for or that seem attractive to me. In other words, I'll maintain control of Jesus' agenda for me, and I'll keep my distance from anyone who might threaten my autonomy."[208] The disconnect that this thinking brings leaves the believer with a false sense of their spiritual growth.[209]

The church must have a clear disciple-making strategy and purpose. Without these, the church devolves into program-centered, disciple-making. These ministry programs—"no matter how well intentioned the design—prove ineffective. Why? Because the programs keep people occupied but not developed enough to experience the rewards and responsibilities spiritual maturity brings."[210] That does not mean that programs are not beneficial. They can add to a disciple's spiritual development. However, these programs

miss the central ingredient in discipleship. Each disciple is a unique individual who grows at a rate peculiar to him or her. Unless disciples receive personal attention so that their particular growth needs are addressed in a way that calls them to die to self and live fully to Christ, a disciple will not be made.[211]

Huizing mentions that the life of a disciple is not just learning or knowledge, "but it is a whole-life surrendering of self for Christ's service."[212] Whole-life surrendering is possible only in relationship-based discipleship.

Relationship with God and Self

Understanding the true nature of being a disciple is vital to a disciple's comprehension of their relationship with God. God says, "Let us make humanity in our image" and in the next verse He creates humanity in His image (Gen 1:26-27). This presents "the first indication of a profound reality that threads its way through all the rest of the biblical story. We are persons created in the image of God."[213] Diane Chandler explains how "God's making humans in the *imago Dei,* followed by Christ's redeeming work on the cross [is] the ultimate expression of love for fallen humanity and the Holy Spirit's ongoing empowerment to live a godly life."[214] The disciple's relationship with God and understanding of self comes from the *imago Dei.*[215]

It is in this recognition that the disciples' inner life is formed. Bill Clem writes that "Gospel identity for us lies in having a renewed image as images of God. Through the work of the Holy Spirit, God allows himself to be seen by us and through us. He graces us with letting us be part of his story."[216] Growth for the disciple involves living life in the renewed image of God. That is, it "means living [a] fully human life in this world in union with Jesus Christ and growing in conformity to his image."[217] Discipleship occurs in relationship with a covenant-keeping God and His creation.[218]

The disciple is called to a relationship with God. Michael Wilkins posits that

> The roots of discipleship go deep into the fertile soil of God's calling. That calling is expressed in the pattern of divine initiative and human response that constitutes the heart of the biblical concept of covenant, manifested in the recurrent promise, 'I will be your God, and you will be my people.'[219]

Disciples heed the call to a covenant relationship with God. God desires to transform the disciple by the renewing of his or her inner being or mind (Rom 12:2). The teachings that the disciples follow "will conflict with cultural values and worldly standards, but the disciple is committed to holding on to the teachings of the master he follows, no matter the cost."[220] The inner being becomes attuned to God through the formed relationship.[221]

Relationship with Others: Believers and Unbelievers

Jesus taught the disciples about love and then showed His love when He gave His life. He taught His disciples that the world would know who they followed if they loved one another: "A new commandment I give to you, that you love one another: just as I have loved you, you also are to love one another. By this all people will know that you are my disciples, if you have love for one another" (John 13:34-35). Christ-followers

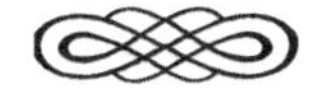

The love that Jesus had for His disciples was unconditional. It is this manner of love He expects His disciples to have for one another.

are not just to act like they love one another; they are commanded to love one another. Part of the disciple-making process is learning to live in loving relationships.

The love that Jesus had for His disciples was unconditional. It is this manner of love He expects His disciples to have for one another. The relationship between disciples must be centered on Christ-commanded love. Ray Anderson writes that the core of "human relations is love."[222] This love requires human relationships between disciples who entrust their lives to each other. The Apostle Paul wrote, "Owe no one anything, except to love each other, for the one who loves another has fulfilled the law … Love does no wrong to a neighbor; therefore love is the fulfillment of the law" (Rom 13:8, 10). This "love seeks the empowerment of others as a positive effect, not power over them."[223] The results of love can be seen in discipleship praxis. Macelaru concludes that "discipleship as social practice can be described as the process within which one (the disciple) becomes as another (the master) empowers him/her to reach his/her full potential."[224] Relationship development among believers is thus foundational to discipleship.

The growth of relationships between believers is fundamental to disciple-making. Spiritual growth needs to be done in the relationship aspect. Although there are parts of the spiritual growth process that can be done on an individual basis, the obligation that disciples have to one another is paramount. Logan and Ridley make this distinction:

> Discipleship in isolation doesn't work. We need others to provide feedback and challenge. We need others to be sounding-boards for our processing. We need others to help us listen to God and to help us understand where he wants us to grow. We need others to help us find a strategy for growth that will work for us. We need others to help steer us back on the right track when we begin to veer off course, become disobedient, and miss the mark in our lives. Change occurs in the context of relationships—and Jesus himself modeled its importance. The fundamental nature of discipleship is relational.[225]

The disciple matures in a community environment where believers work in harmony to help each other in their spiritual journeys.[226] The author of Proverbs wrote, "Iron sharpens iron, and one man sharpens another" (27:17). Iron rubbing against iron sharpens the iron. That is the way relationships work amongst believers. Disciples sharpen and shape the lives of those around them in the process of discipleship.

The believer's relationship with other believers is vital. The believer's relationship to unbelievers is equally vital. It is significant that believers understand that "the gospel came to you because it was heading to someone else. God never intended for your salvation to be an end, but a beginning. God saved you to be a conduit through whom His glorious, life-changing gospel would flow to others."[227] The church must be involved with those who are unbelievers. In this involvement, "a community of disciples needs to engage with the world through the language they understand. By so doing, it is hoped that the disciples will be able to touch and disciple the world that they attempt to reach."[228] Barna and Kinnaman concur and state that the life-changing message of Jesus presents the Christian community with "an obligation to understand the unchurched."[229] Healthy relationships must be refined and become an outgrowth of the church's spiritual maturity.

The number of unchurched individuals in America culture is estimated to be 60-70 percent of the population. These unchurched persons "have little to no understanding or appreciation of those church words, hymns, and religious rituals we have been and are nurtured by."[230] This presents a great challenge to the church and individual believers.[231] The call to make disciples involves more than just believers in the church. Also, "when a church evangelizes with a penetration strategy of ongoing love, relationship, and service, it's much tougher for non-Christians to ignore the church's gospel message."[232] The gospel is the good news of salvation to all who believe. In order to share this good news, the disciple must be in the world but not of the world.

Ralph Moore identifies that "the disciple-making process starts before someone chooses to walk with the Lord. To accomplish this part of the journey, you must hangout with pre-Christians. If you only spend time with Christ-followers, a fair-sized part of your personal circle of concern will remain hell-bound."[233] Developing relationships with the unchurched, unbelievers, and pre-Christians is vital in following the command in the Great Commission.[234]

Relationships in Daily Life: Calling and Work

Paul wrote to the churches in Ephesus about how they were to live their daily lives. He admonished them to "look carefully then how you walk, not as unwise but as wise, making the best use of the time, because the days are evil" (Eph 5:15-16). Paul wanted the believers to understand the weightiness of living daily for Christ. The standard that believers must live by affects every area of their lives. Vocational clarity is in line with the concept of daily living. The term *vocation* comes from the Latin word for "calling." Gene Veith explains that "the Scripture is full of passages that describe how we have been called to faith through the Gospel (e.g., 2 Thessalonians 2:14), how God *calls* us to a particular office or a way of life (1 Corinthians 1:1-2; 7:15-20)."[235] It is in one's calling or vocation that faith is lived out.[236] Steven Garber describes vocation as "having to address the wholeness of life, the range of relationships and responsibilities. Work, yes, but also families, and neighbors, and citizenship, locally and globally—all of this and more is seen as vocation."[237] Garber also notes that vocation is not the same as occupation.[238] Daily work is included in vocation but is more than work. Each disciple has been given gifts and talents to use in Christ's service.

Another aspect of the disciple's relationships in daily life is found in the "workplace and participation in the economy (where goods and services are exchanged to supply the needs of our communities)."[239] It is in this context where disciples "live out the Great Commission (Mt. 28:18-20; Acts 1:8), the Great Commandment (Mt. 22:37:37-40) and our personal mission."[240] The disciples' mission field is the marketplace. *Work* can be defined as "meaningful activity that adds value to the household economy."[241] All work that disciples do is God-honoring work. If the believers "will look at our work through the lens of Holy Scripture, our work, no matter what we have been called to do, is imbued with great meaning and significance."[242] Believers' contributions to the economy are vital. God's desire is for His disciples to be good stewards of what He has given and participants in local and global economy.

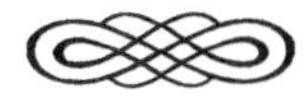

The disciples' mission field is the marketplace.

Summary

Wilkins explains how the Great Commission "indicated that the outcome of conversion to Christianity is that a person becomes a disciple of Jesus. Therefore, all Christians are disciples of Jesus."[243] All believers are disciples. Therefore, all believers are to fulfill the command of the Great Commission with their lives. Disciple-making requires intentionality to build relationships with God, other believers, and unbelievers. This is accomplished through the power of the Holy Spirit (Acts 1:8).

6.

Whole-Life Disciple-Making
Exemplified in Two Dimensions[296]

Disciples are to display God to the world through their daily lives. Paul writes to the churches in Corinth that disciples have the mind of Christ (1 Cor 2:15). Vanhoozer explains:

> This is an extraordinary declaration, whether one reads it as making a theological or a psychological claim. The apostle Paul is not simply saying that we have the same beliefs, much less the same brainwaves, as the historical Jesus. Disciples are neither carbon nor cerebral copies of Christ. In context, Paul is explaining to the Corinthians why the wise men of this age do not understand the wisdom of God: they cannot accept, or even comprehend, the thoughts of God, much less the wisdom of the cross, because they do not have the Spirit of God (1 Cor 2:11).[244]

It is not only super spiritual disciples who have the mind of Christ: it is all disciples. All disciples are to exemplify Christ in disciple-making relationships. Two of the five dimensions of these relationships are spiritual formation and personal wholeness. Disciples should understand that "Discipleship is a life-long process in which we allow the Holy Spirit to form us into the image of Christ."[245] Spirit-empowered discipleship is the heartbeat of the Church.

Spiritual Formation

The first dimension of discipleship is spiritual formation. This is

It is not only super spiritual disciples who have the mind of Christ: it is all disciples.

the foundation of discipleship. Spiritual formation "is the dimension that most people associate with the concept of discipleship, and rightly so. It is the critical starting point for our journey with Christ."[246] In spiritual formation, believers take on the character of Christ by being conformed to His image. This takes place from the inside out.

Spiritual formation is when "the disciple positions himself [or herself] to follow Jesus. The actual process of reforming, or spiritual formation, involves both God's grace and the individual's efforts."[247] Spiritual formation is more than a one-time event, rather it is a "continual process of transforming the whole person, including the healing of woundedness and rebellion, by the power of God, not to be confused with mere technique or program."[248] Disciples must lay a solid spiritual foundation for their lives and allow the Holy Spirit to transform them daily.

Love the Word of God

God's Word is vital to the disciples' spiritual health. As disciples become "familiar with Scriptures [they] develop a love for reading them and it gives [them] confidence to engage others in discussions that center on the Bible."[249] God's Word "is living and active, sharper than any two-edged sword, piercing to the division of soul and of spirit, of joints and of marrow, and discerning the thoughts and intentions of the heart" (Heb 4:12). Scripture is not just something that disciples memorize, recite, or read; Scripture is alive. It has power to help disciples in their walk with God. Fettke writes that "Any authentic work of God inside believers has to begin with God's Word."[250] All Scripture has meaning and importance in the believers' lives. When disciples allow God's Word to mature them and bloom in them, love for God's Word grows strong (2 Tim 3:15-17).

Pray Without Ceasing

Disciples understand the vital nature of prayer. As they mature, they develop "the capacity to communicate with God continually, regardless of the context that they find themselves in."[251] Jesus gave a pattern for prayer to His disciples:

> Our Father in heaven, hallowed be your name. Your kingdom come, your will be done, on earth as it is in heaven. Give us this day our daily bread, and forgive us our debts, as we also have forgiven our debtors. And lead us not into temptation, but deliver us from evil (Matt 6:9-13).

Maturing disciples "have developed the capacity that Paul speaks about in 1 Thessalonians 5:17, 'pray without ceasing'."[252] Communication with God is vital.

Lilly writes that "the foundation of everything that a disciple does is prayer. It would be a poor foundation to the process of Disciple-Making if it were anything else but prayer."[253] Prayer not only makes disciples aware of who God is but also aware of their own inner lives. It is in this knowledge that Paul encouraged believers to "not be anxious about anything, but in everything by prayer and supplication with thanksgiving let your requests be made known to God" (Phil 4:6). In everything, prayer must be foundational.

Worship in Spirit and Truth

Worship is an integral part of the believers' lives. All "disciples are called to worship God under all circumstances."[254] Jesus, in conversation with the woman at the well, stated that "God is

Prayer not only makes disciples aware of who God is but also aware of their own inner lives.

spirit, and those who worship him must worship in spirit and truth" (John 4:24). The place of worship is not an issue; it is the attitude that matters. True worship comes from the heart. "It is easy to worship when we are in the company of others who are singing God's praises, but it is quite another challenge to be worshipping him when we are working at our job, or when we are not feeling well."[255] Worship is not just an outward expression. Worship is also an expression from the inner self to God.

Listen to the Voice of God

Disciples who are growing "are able to discern the voice of God and differentiate it from all other voices that demand their attention."[256] God speaks, and His disciples learn to hear His voice and follow Him (John 10:27). "This is a skill that is developed over time."[257] Richard Foster notes that in the book of Acts "we see over and over again … God's people learning to live on the basis of hearing God's voice and obeying his word."[258] Disciples learn to understand God's will for them by learning to listen to the voice of God.

Pursue Biblical Principles for Living

Just as love for God's Word is essential, pursuing those biblical principles are vital as well. This is "going beyond just reading the Bible, disciples are on a path to understand how the Scriptures should be applied in daily life."[259] If disciples simply read God's Word and never attempt to apply it to their lives, they will be lacking in growth and understanding in their spiritual lives. Paul wrote that disciples are to be conformed to the image of Christ (Rom 8:29). Bill Hull notes that to be conformed to the image of Christ is to be like Christ. Hull includes six areas of transformation that, when lived out, lead to being conformed to Christ: (1) transformed mind, (2) transformed character, (3) transformed relationships, (4) transformed habits, (5) transformed service, and (6) transformed influence.[260] Disciples are formed, conformed, and transformed by pursuing biblical principles.

Share the Gospel Wisely with Others

Disciples, by nature, should be making new disciples. Sharing their faith with unbelievers is part of their spiritual lives. "Disciples desire to share the Gospel with others in a way that draws people closer to the Gospel rather than pushing them further away."[261] Terry Bowland writes about three basic forms of evangelism that are used today: (1) proclamational evangelism—"formal preaching of the gospel," (2) confrontational/intrusional evangelism—"walking up to a stranger and initiating a presentation of the gospel," and (3) relational/incarnational evangelism—"this occurs when a Christian becomes acquainted with, and eventually becomes friends with, a non-Christian."[262] The relational/incarnational evangelism is where disciples need to live. Bowland further notes that

> The goal of evangelism is not winning people to a particular point of view, although everyone evangelized will develop a point of view. Christ did not send us into the world to champion some great argument, The Great Commission is not, 'Go into all the world and win every theological argument!' We are to win people.[263]

Disciples need to learn to share the gospel wisely in order to be a light to a dark world.

Enjoy Fellowship in the Local Church

Discipleship is not a solo act. Discipleship "is a community experience wherein we allow our brothers and sisters in the faith to speak into our lives."[264] The need for fellowship within the confines of relationship to God and other Christians is what allows growth to occur. Disciples need one another and understand that the "one-anothers are not optional for the Christian life. They are community-building mandates from God for his people."[265] Fellowship with other disciples is more than weekly attendance at a church service, though that is imperative. True fellowship is the "motivation to pursue this communal experience with other Christians and to maintain contact with your brothers and sisters in the Christian community."[266] The simplicity of fellowship and the necessity of community are what should make the local church appealing.

Cultivate Solitude

Solitude is not just being alone. Rather, it is "sitting quietly and pondering the character and works of our God."[267] Ruth Barton surmises that "in solitude we are rescued from relentless human striving to solve the challenges of ministry through intellectual achievements and hard work, so that we can experience the life of the Spirit guiding toward that true way that lies between one polarity and another."[268] Solitude is something that Jesus practiced (Luke 6:12). Solitude "enable[s] us to experience a place of authenticity within and to invite God to meet us there."[269] Pondering the mighty acts of God and His wonders is a powerful discipline.[270]

Personal Wholeness

The second dimension of discipleship is personal wholeness. This dimension "places attention on the realities in our own hearts, issues that reveal the level of emotional health."[271] Jesus told His disciples that they should love their neighbors as themselves

(Mark 12:31). Paul wrote, "For no one ever hated his own flesh, but nourishes and cherishes it" (Eph 5:29). Therefore, "reasonable self-care is part of being whole."[272] Chandler goes on to define emotional wellness, writing that "emotional formation concerns the capacity to identify, understand, express and reflect upon one's own and other's feelings, desires and passions in healthy and God-honoring ways."[273] Concerning this, Paul wrote that believers should let the peace of Christ rule their hearts (Col 3:15).

Work on Your Physical Health

Being physically fit is something towards which disciples should strive. Paul wrote that believer's bodies are the temple or house of the Holy Spirit (1 Cor 6:19). It is proper then to note that "our bodies have replaced the Tabernacle in the Wilderness of the Old Testament as the place where God resides and in the new Covenant our bodies become that place. It therefore makes sense that we are admonished to take care of our bodies."[274] Paul wrote about the usefulness of keeping his physical body in good shape to further the kingdom (1 Cor 9:24-27).

Develop a Positive Self-Image

Disciples need to develop a healthy self-image of who they are in Christ. Such an image is not simply self-value or self-worth but rather understanding that they are made in the image of God (Gen 1:26-28). Disciples "need to be able to look in the mirror each day and not only be comfortable, but [also] rejoice in what they see."[275] Bill Clem posits that "'image of God' is a meaningless description without a God to image. What's worse is when people miss the point that they are God's image bearers and elevate being human as an ultimate calling. To leave God out of the picture means to sabotage our chance to image him."[276] Ultimately, disciples know that they are God's handiwork, created for good works in Christ (Eph 2:10).

Nurture Gratitude

Maturing disciples learn to be grateful in every situation. They "are grateful people rejoicing in the profound, undeserved blessings they enjoy every day."[277] Paul wrote to the church in Thessalonica that they were to give thanks in all circumstances (1 Thess 5:18). Gratitude in all situations is a spiritual discipline that needs cultivation. Chandler writes that "our entire lives are to be an expression of reverence and gratefulness to God for creating us, saving us and giving us a future and a hope."[278] Giving thanks is a sign of spiritual maturation.

Manage Negative Emotions

God created humanity with emotions. Each day, disciples experience a wide range of emotions from anger to happiness, frustration to fear, even embarrassment. "These emotions typically trigger responses that are either normal or sinful. Learning to manage our negative emotions is one of the discipleship tasks that the Holy Spirit helps us with."[279] Karen Lawson expresses the effect that negative emotions can have on people. She writes,

> Negative attitudes and feelings of helplessness and hopelessness can create chronic stress, which upsets the body's hormone balance, depletes the brain chemicals required for happiness, and damages the immune system. Chronic stress can actually decrease our lifespan. (Science has now identified that stress shortens our telomeres, the "end caps" of our DNA strands, which causes us to age more quickly.)[280]

Disciples, through the leading of the Holy Spirit, "[foster] affections of joy, peace and patience when negative emotions flood in to make us gloomy and sad."[281] Paul wrote that cultivating the fruit of the Spirit helps disciples to develop emotions that are authentic in Christ.

Hope for the Future

Hope, for the disciples of Christ, has at its source the resurrection of Jesus. Concerning this hope, Carpenter and Comfort explain that

> The Greek term *elpis* denotes "confident expectation" or "anticipation"—not "wishful thinking." Hope is consequently an expectation or belief in the fulfillment of God's promises, Biblical hope is hope in what God will do in the future. At the heart of Christian hope is the resurrection of Jesus.[282]

In Christ's resurrection, His followers have a preview of their future.[283] "Learning to live in faith when we don't know what the future might bring or what could happen to us as everything changes, is a sign of a mature disciple of Christ."[284] The present and future are in God's hands, and growing disciples understand they are secure in Him.

Keep a Clean Conscience

Disciples learn to deal with "spiritual attacks against their inner well-being (2 Cor 10:1-6)."[285] These attacks come from the spiritual enemy and generally focus on an individual's past. They attempt to rob believers of their peace that comes from God.[286] A clean conscience is formed by a disciple "developing a peace in their hearts about their past."[287] John wrote concerning a clean conscience: "Beloved, if our heart does not condemn us, we have confidence before God; and whatever we ask we receive from him, because we keep his commandments and do what pleases him" (1 John 3:22-23). Letting go of the past can lead to a peace that allows a disciple to live with a clean conscience.

Hone Self-Discipline

The fruit of the Spirit (Gal 5:22-23) is what the Holy Spirit is cultivating in disciples' lives.[288] Self-discipline is one of those fruits. "Research provides us with insights into the benefits of delayed gratification. Being able to postpone immediate gratification in order to enjoy a greater reward later has been associated with a wide variety of mental, emotional, and physical benefits."[289] Peter encouraged his hearers to rejoice even though they may be going through trials. The later reward is worth the present suffering (1 Pet 1:6ff). Reigning in impulses through the power of the Holy Spirit brings about the self-discipline that leads to growth.

Manage Personal Resources

Being a good steward of resources, income, and debt commitments "are excellent barometers of spiritual maturity. When money becomes so important that it enslaves us to work too many hours a week, or we live beyond our means, we are in a zone of spiritual danger."[290] Learning to manage personal resources frees disciples to owe no one anything except to love one another (Rom 13:8-10).

Disciples are to exemplify Christ in their daily lives. The life-long process of spiritual formation and personal wholeness, empowered by the Holy Spirit, aids the disciples in their growth as representatives of Christ. As these outcomes are synthesized into daily living, they encourage maturity and growth in disciples' lives.

Conclusion to Part Two

Discipleship is the call to live life as pleasing to Jesus. Relationships are a vital part of living that life including the disciple's relationship with God, other disciples, and unbelievers. The command to make disciples cannot be ignored or parsed out in program-form. The gospel "embeds in its command to 'go and make disciples' the measurement of the movement's health. By Christ's own words, this is the simplest gauge we use to measure success or failure. Are we making disciples?"[291] Disciples must be growing the inner-self while reaching out to the unbeliever. Minho Song notes the appropriate context for reaching out. He writes,

> Discipleship in context rises out of a dynamic interplay between text (passed down by tradition) and context. By paying attention to both the Bible and the context in which people live, we are then able to bring the task of disciple-making in a culturally relevant and biblically faithful manner.[292]

Disciples must be intentional about the command to make disciples and understand the context within which they are to live. Being engaged with like-minded disciples on their journey and proclaiming the good news to a lost world is the discipleship God desires. Flourishing in Christ is a "long obedience in the same direction."[293]

PART THREE

The material in Part Three will assist pastors and church leaders in mobilizing their congregations and ministries for a process of embracing a whole-life discipleship model, which produces disciples who make disciples.

Based on my biblical and professional research on whole-life discipleship, the material in this section allows for an eleven-week teaching series (The Appendix includes YouTube videos of my eleven weeks of teaching plus Session notes for eight weeks.) on spiritual formation and personal wholeness, which can be adapted to assist leaders in various practical ministry opportunities (such as leadership training, small group studies, sermon presentation, etc.) or to empower individual believers devotionally as they begin their journey of being disciples who make disciples.

Beginning the
Conversation

7.

The following questionnaire can be utilized to help stimulate conversation and thoughtfulness about discipleship in a local church setting.

I AM A DISCIPLE BY CHOICE…

1) How would you best define the term disciple?

    a. Learner

    b. Christian

    c. Believer

    d. Follower

2) Is there a difference between a Christian and a Disciple?

    YES or NO

    Explain: ____

____

____

____

3) What are the best ways to disciple others? Circle all that apply.

    a. Small Groups

    b. Sports Team

    c. Bible Study

    d. Starbucks

    e. One-on-One

    f. Qdoba

    g. Sunday school

    h. Weekend Retreat

    i. Texting/IM

4) What are the best discipleship tools? _______________________

____

____

____

____

5) Can unbelievers be disciples?

    YES or NO

6) Can unbelievers be discipled?

    YES or NO

7) Where does most discipleship take place?

    a. Church

    b. Home

    c. Marketplace

    d. Work

8) How were you discipled? _______________________

____

____

____

____

9) Would you consider yourself a disciple-maker?
    YES or NO

10) Are you currently in a discipling situation?
    YES or NO_

8.

Taking the
DD Assessment

The Discipleship Dynamics Assessment online tool is a next practical step you can take in the process of whole-life discipleship. The DD license for this tool is available for purchase here: Discipleshipdynamics.com.[294] Getting a group account allows the use of the assessment as well as provides future use for a church. The online assessment is designed for *individuals* to use and is personal in nature. It allows the users to see their individual scores and allows the leadership to see all the scores *as a total group*. The privacy feature is a great bonus for participants. The assessment gives participants a look at their lives related to discipleship in the DD dimensions and outcomes.

9. *Discipleship* Curriculum

This chapter contains curriculum (including YouTube videos of the sessions and PowerPoints) that I developed for *two* of the five Discipleship Dynamics domains/ dimensions and *sixteen* of the thirty-five outcomes. I based the lessons on my biblical-theological and professional research as well as Scriptures that coincide with the sixteen outcomes.

This curriculum is designed for eleven sessions but is adaptable to numerous ministry settings The Session notes that follow provide content for an eight-week study._I recommend that as facilitator, you begin each week with prayer and then recap the previous lesson before providing any further reading recommendations on the particular outcomes to be discussed that week. The questionnaire discussed in chapter 7 of this book can either be utilized *prior* to the teaching sessions to give both facilitator and participants a sense of their own understanding about discipleship prior to the first session, or it could be utilized at the beginning of the very first session as an icebreaker.

The following are YouTube video uploads of the eleven teaching sessions that I conducted. This material is free as a resource to you in adapting this material to your own setting(s):

YouTube Videos of Teaching Sessions

Lesson 1 https://youtu.be/KOsY7PkurMQ

Lesson 2 https://youtu.be/zXaJrGGboQI

Lesson 3 https://youtu.be/Jq27aO9bBwM

Lesson 4 https://youtu.be/AZOypbLvoww

Lesson 5 https://youtu.be/jKiopzTpggI

Lesson 6 https://youtu.be/T8j5GckSZK8

Lesson 7 https://youtu.be/dpMWW2V0CCs

Lesson 8 https://youtu.be/CXlSTfKMC3A

Lesson 9 https://youtu.be/roXZ7TlU6nA

Lesson 10 https://youtu.be/RGAON80OnK0

Lesson 11 https://youtu.be/jmTxesU1mLg

Teaching Outline

Session 1

"No one accidently creates disciples. Discipleship is an intentional pursuit" (Mike Breen, *Building a Discipleship Culture*, 20).

Definitions

Disciple - "Someone who follows another person or another way of life and who submits himself [or herself] to the discipline (teaching) of that leader or way" (P. Helm, *Baker Encyclopedia of the Bible,* vol. 1, 629).

Discipleship - "The process of becoming a committed follower of Jesus Christ, with all the spiritual discipline and benefits which this brings" (M. H. Manser, *Dictionary of Bible Themes*).

Discipling - "Discipling is an intentional relationship in which we walk alongside other disciples in order to encourage, equip and challenge one another in love to grow toward maturity in Christ. This includes equipping the disciple to teach others as well" (Greg Ogden, *Discipleship Essentials,* 17).

"Discipleship is the life-long process in which we allow the Holy Spirit to form us into the image of Christ. This process involves our spiritual formation, the development of personal wholeness, healthy relationships, and vocational clarity. The purpose of these Spirit-empowered changes is that the disciple would be able to more adequately manifest the character of Christ in their workplace and in their community with such clarity and power that the world would gain a tangible glimpse of the Kingdom of God in action as they interact with this disciple" (Discipleship Dynamics).

Scriptures

Matthew 28:18-20

Luke 9:23

Acts 11:25-26

Mark 1:16-20

Luke 9:57-62

John 10:27

Examples of discipling in Scripture

Moses and Joshua (Num 27:18-20)

Elijah and Elisha (1 Kgs 19:19-21)

Jesus and the Apostles (Mark 3:14-15)

Barnabas and Paul (Acts 9:27; 11:22-26)

Barnabas and John Mark (Acts 15:37-39)

Paul and Timothy (2 Tim 2:2).

Session 2

"Disciple making ensures that the Gospel is embedded deeply in the lives of mature believers who serve as links to the future" (Greg Ogden, *Discipleship Essentials*, 21).

"The emphasis in discipleship must shift from information to transformation. Information downloading is easy. In contrast, transformational living doesn't require huge amounts of information, but it does require the consistent practice of what you know" (Bob Roberts, Jr., *Transformation*, 69).

"Discipleship is not only about knowledge (2 Peter 3:18); it's about character, behavior, attitudes, a posture of humility, teachability—and grace for continued growth. Knowledge may be a building block, but it's not enough on its own. By itself, knowledge puffs up. The heart of discipleship displays Jesus to those around us in a way that they can see. If there's something real on the inside, it needs to be observable on the outside. Inner qualities can only be seen through behaviors" (Robert Logan and Charles Ridley, *The Discipleship Difference*, 25).

"Discipleship isn't a random assortment of facts and propositions and behaviors; discipleship is something that is you to the core and is completely incarnated in you. If it is information, it is information that has worked its way into you and is now part of you, in the same way that John talks about the *Logos* being wrapped up in the person of Jesus: 'the Word became flesh'" (Mike Breen, *Building a Discipling Culture*, 28).

"Discipleship in isolation doesn't work. We need others to provide feedback and challenge. We need others to be sounding-boards for our processing. We need others to help us listen to God and to help us understand where he wants us to grow. We need others to help us find a strategy for growth that will work for us. We need others to steer us back on the right track when we begin to veer off course, become disobedient, and miss the mark in our lives. Change occurs in the context of relationships- and Jesus himself modeled its importance. The fundamental nature of discipleship is relational" (Robert Logan and Charles Ridley, *The Discipleship Difference*, 7).

Session 3

Ten Principles That Reflect How Jesus Made Disciples

(Robert Logan and Charles Ridley, *The Discipleship Difference: Making Disciples While Growing as Disciples*, 14-18.)

1. Jesus made disciples of ordinary people, not superstars.

    Lesson for us: Discipleship is for everyone. It's not the fast track or the honors course- it's for ordinary people … everyone!

2. Jesus started with unbelievers and made disciples outside the church.

    Lesson for us: People don't have to be Christians to begin the journey of discipleship, just willing to explore.

3. Jesus expected that his disciples would make disciples.

    Lesson for us: Being sent out to make more disciples is a given. It's what disciples do.

4. Jesus made disciples within the context of relationships.

    Lesson for us: Pay attention to the people around you, in your natural network of relationships.

5. Jesus skewed discipleship toward the practical rather than the academic.

    Lesson for us: Whenever you have a choice between hands-on learning and classroom learning, go with hands-on learning. It sticks better anyway!

6. Jesus took people where they were at and started there.

   Lesson for us: Never count anyone out as a potential disciple. Remember that "whosoever will" may come, as an invitation of the gospel of grace.

7. Jesus dealt with people differently at different times of their lives.

   Lesson for us: Be flexible. Even the same person needs different input and types of feedback at different times in their lives of discipleship.

8. Jesus recognized and accepted that discipleship is a process, complete with setbacks.

   Lesson for us: Everybody has weaknesses, and everybody fails sometimes. That doesn't mean they are not disciples.

9. Jesus assumed discipleship to be holistic in nature, touching on and transforming all areas of life.

   Lesson for us: Discipleship will impact every area of a person's life- not just the "spiritual" parts.

10. Jesus intended for disciple-making to continue through the generations, multiplying across cultures.

    Lesson for us: Disciple-making is what Jesus wants us to focus on until His return, without any regard to geography, race, language, culture, or generation.

Session 4

The Distinguishing Marks of a Disciple
(Bill Hull, *Complete Book of Discipleship*, 113-152)

Six-Fold Definition of Being Conformed to the Image of Christ

1. Transformed Mind: Believing as Jesus Believed (Rom 12:2)

2. Transformed Character: Live the Way Jesus Lived (Matt 4:1-10)

3. Transformed Relationships: Love the Way Jesus Loved (John 13:34-35)

4. Transformed Habits: Train the Way Jesus Trained (Luke 2:41-52)

5. Transformed Service: Minister as Jesus Ministered (Mark 10:45)

6. Transformed Influence: Lead the Way Jesus Led (Phil 2:5-11)

Session 5

"Disciples desire to share the Gospel with others in a way that draws people closer to the Gospel rather than pushing them further away. Sharing wisely means we can convey the Gospel story and our testimony with clarity and humility" (Discipleship Dynamics).

Ed Stetzer, Lifeway Research (*Influence Magazine*)

- 72% of unchurched people believe the church "is full of hypocrites"

- 78% said they would be willing to listen to someone who wants to share what they believe about Christianity

- Protestant Churchgoers - "In the past six months, about how many times have you personally shared with someone how to become a Christian?"

0	61%
1	16%
2	9%
3	3%
4	2%
5	2%
6-10	4%
11-15	1%
16+	1%

- Protestant Churchgoers - "In the past six months, about how many times have you personally invited an unchurched person to attend church?"

0	44%
1	17%
2	11%

3	6%
4	8%
5	6%
6-10	6%
11-15	0%
16+	2%

- "I believe the enemy's primary strategy against the Church is not to turn pastors toward deviant sin or errant theology, but to distract us with (seemingly) good commissions that pull us away from the Great Commission."

- "Events, sermons series and children's programs honor God. But in the absence of your congregation reaching friends and neighbors for Jesus, programs are idols that take the place of the Great Commission."

"The healthy disciple maximizes every opportunity to share the love of Christ, in word and deed, with those outside the faith" (Stephen Macchia, *Becoming a Healthy Disciple*, 146).

"One reason that we're so reluctant to evangelize is because we believe that evangelism is imposing ourselves on others and leaving people cowering, feeling unimportant, used, and violated. We equate evangelism with selling. We see ourselves like those annoying phone solicitors who always seem to call us when we're sitting down to dinner! For this reason, many of us run from anything that resembles evangelism. Sharing your faith doesn't impose itself on others, leaving them feeling resentful and used. It invites people to step beyond a superficial friendship where no one really cares about listening, and to head toward deep spiritual relationship" (John Leonard, *Getting Real: Sharing Your Everyday Faith Every Day*).

Session 6

Personal Characteristics of Disciples

(Bill Hull, *Complete Book of Discipleship*, 47)

John 15:7-13

1. A disciple abides in Christ through the Word and prayer (v. 7).

2. A disciple bears much fruit (v. 8).

3. A disciple responds to God's love with obedience (vv. 9-10).

4. A disciple possesses joy (v. 11).

5. A disciple loves as Christ loved (vv. 12-13).

Session 7

Purpose of Discipleship

(Bill Hull, *Choose the Life: Exploring a Faith that Embraces Discipleship*, 36-42)

> "The purpose of discipleship is to go deeper with God, to be shaped into the image of Christ, because character is developed in community. If we are following the New Testament model, discipleship should look like this today:

1. A disciple submits to a teacher who teaches him or her how to follow Jesus.

2. A disciple learns Jesus' words.

3. A disciple learns Jesus' ways of ministry.

4. A disciple imitates Jesus' life and character.

5. A disciple finds and teaches other disciples for Jesus."

Session 8

What Discipleship is Not....

(Robert Gallaty, *Rediscovering Discipleship*, 155-156)

- It's not a class.

- It's not a seminar.

- It's not a degree you earn.

- It's not a program.

- It's not a 12-week Bible study.

- It's not a 40-day home group.

- It's not a quick process.

- It's not a quick fix.

- It's not reserved for Super Christians.

- It's not hard.

- It's not an option.

What it is...

- Discipleship is intentionally equipping believers with the Word of God through accountable relationships empowered by the Holy Spirit in order to replicate faithful followers of Christ.

- When people become disciples, they learn what Jesus said and live out what Jesus did.

Conclusion to Part Three

In utilizing the teaching material in this book, participants can be presented with the opportunity to learn, re-learn, and participate in moving the local church to focus outwardly by looking inward. The lessons are designed to aid in this transformation. This material has had a profound impact on my life regarding the spiritual disciplines required of disciples of Christ. I trust that it will also make a lasting contribution to move your ministry forward in the community where you serve.

In this process, participants can gain a deeper understanding of what it means to be a disciple growing in the power of the Holy Spirit. The follower of Christ is at once and always a disciple. Spiritual growth is a lifelong responsibility of the disciple in cooperation with the Holy Spirit. Growth does not cease. There is no end to the maturation process of the disciple.

Second, participants can develop a greater understanding of the whole-life concept of what it means to be a disciple. There is no delineation between "Christian," "believer," and "disciple." The necessity of whole-life growth through all the spiritual disciplines needs to become a deeper part of disciples' lives, not just in one or two disciplines. This will create a hunger for deeper relationship with Christ.

Finally, the participants can engage in expanding their relationship with Christ, with other disciples, and with unbelievers. These lessons can give them the tools to use in this pursuit. The dire need for Christ seen in the world today can compel participants to move in the direction of community transformation, which will assist both the church and the lives of these individuals.

Appendix

Recommendations for Future Study

The material presented in this book does not exhaust the depth of discipleship and making disciples. As a result, there are several recommendations for future study on the subject. First, I recommend finding a way to take the many terms currently in use and develop a list of definitions for those terms to simplify and standardize Christian understanding of them. In my research, for example, the term *spiritual formation* was used in various ways dependent on the author's understanding. This led to some confusion among the participants in my project. If there can be research done and a consensus formed, much confusion concerning discipleship could be made clear.

Second, there needs to be more research done concerning discipleship from the Old Testament perspective. There are abounding numbers of books, academic writings, and articles centered on the Great Commission and the Gospels. There are also several writings, although less, on the subject of discipleship as developed from Paul's writings and the General Epistles. However, there was a dearth of information from the Old Testament writings. I believe a deeper look at the principles of discipleship via the Old Testament would aid in a greater understanding of the discipleship to which Jesus called all Christians.

Third, I see a need for more writing and training on the practical side of discipleship. Pastors and leaders often attend cookie-cutter seminars on discipleship that they are expected to take back to their churches and implement as is. However, every church and every pastor is different. Putting into practice principles of discipleship is a subject that needs to be fleshed out and developed for churches of every size and context.

Last, I would like to see more tools similar to the Discipleship Dynamics Assessment developed for measuring discipleship. I know this would be a difficult task. The truth is that churches measure what is valued. Attendance, offering, membership, water baptisms, salvations, baptism in the Holy Spirit, etc., are measured and, therefore, valued. Churches need to continue to find ways to measure discipleship. If these kinds of tools can be put into pastors' and leaders' hands, this would be a tremendous aid to them in leading their congregations.

Glossary

Disciple. Learner; characterized by thoughts that are accompanied by endeavor.

Discipleship Dynamics Assessment. A biblical, comprehensive, practical assessment offering individuals and churches clear understanding of the effectiveness of their current discipleship strategy. This assessment offers a glimpse into the five dimensions of discipleship that includes insights on thirty-five outcomes within the five dimensions.

Great Commission. Jesus's final instructions and primary command, found in Matthew 28:16-20 and Mark 4:15, to make disciples of all nations.

Personal Wholeness. "Places attention on the realities in our own hearts, issues that reveal the level of emotional health."[295]

Relationships. Ultimately, disciple-making is about relationships with unbelievers, other believers, and God.

Spiritual Formation. The process of spiritual shaping and growth.

Transformational. Both the starting point and the goal of spiritual formation and discipleship is to be changed to the image of Christ.

Whole-life Discipleship. Learners taking seriously what it means to follow Jesus and represent Him in the context of one's life.

Recommended Resources

Barna, George and David Kinnaman. *Churchless: Understanding Today's Unchurched and How to Connect with Them.* Carol Stream, IL: Tyndale Momentum, 2014.

Bennett, Ron. *Intentional Disciplemaking: Cultivating Spiritual Maturity in the Local Church.* Colorado Springs, CO: NavPress, 2001.

Bonhoeffer, Dietrich. *Cost of Discipleship.* New York: Touchstone, 1995.

Breen, Mike, and the 3DM Team. *Building a Discipling Culture: How to Release a Missional Movement by Discipling People Like Jesus Did.* N.p.: 3DM Publishing, 2011.

Chandler, Diane J. *Christian Spiritual Formation: An Integrated Approach for Personal and Relational Wholeness.* Downers Grove, IL: IVP Academic, 2014.

Discipleship Dynamics, LLC. *Discipleship Dynamics: Discover, Define, Disciple.* 2016. Accessed February 7, 2018. https://discipleshipdynamics.com/.

Early, Dave, and Rod Dempsey. *Disciple Making Is ... How to Live the Great Commission with Passion and Confidence.* Nashville, TN: B&H Publishing Group, 2013.

Gallaty, Robby. *Growing Up: How to be a Disciple Who Makes Disciples.* Nashville, TN: B&H Publishing Group, 2013.

Rediscovering Discipleship: Making Jesus' Final Words Our First Work Grand Rapids, MI: Zondervan, 2015.

Geiger, Eric, Michael Kelley, and Philip Nation. *Transformational Discipleship: How People Really Grow.* Nashville, TN: B&H Publishing Group, 2012.

Hammett, Edward H. *Reframing Spiritual Formation: Discipleship in an Unchurched Culture.* Macon, GA: Smith & Helwys Publishing Incorporated, 2002.

Harrington, Bobby, and Alex Absalom. *Discipleship That Fits: The Five Kinds of Relationships God Uses to Help Us Grow.* Grand Rapids, MI: Zondervan, 2016.

Harrington, Bobby, and Josh Patrick. *The Disciple Maker's Handbook: 7 Elements of a Discipleship Lifestyle.* Grand Rapids, MI: Zondervan, 2017.

Hull, Bill. *Choose the Life: Exploring a Faith That Embraces Discipleship.* Grand Rapids, MI: Baker Books, 2004.

Conversion & Discipleship: You Can't Have One Without the Other. Grand Rapids, MI: Zondervan, 2016.

Jesus Christ Disciplemaker. Grand Rapids, MI: Baker Books, 2007.

The Complete Book of Discipleship: On Being and Making Followers of Christ. Colorado Springs, CO: NavPress, 2006.

The Disciple-Making Church: Leading a Body of Believers on the Journey of Faith. Grand Rapids, MI: Baker Books, 2010.

Logan, Robert E., and Charles R. Ridley. *The Discipleship Difference: Making Disciples While Growing as Disciples.* San Bernardino, CA: Logan Leadership, 2016.

Malphurs, Aubrey. *Strategic Disciplemaking: A Practical Tool for Successful Ministry.* Grand Rapids, MI: Baker Books, 2009.

McNabb, Bob. *Spiritual Multiplication in the Real World: Why Some Disciple-Makers Reproduce When Others Fail.* N.p.: Multiplication Press, 2013.

Moore, Ralph. *Making Disciples: Developing Lifelong Followers of Jesus.* Ventura, CA: Regal Books, 2012.

Ogden, Greg. *Transforming Discipleship: Making Disciples a Few at a Time.* Downers Grove, IL: InterVarsity Press, 2003.

Osborne, Larry. *Mission Creep: The 5 Subtle Shifts that Sabotage Evangelism & Discipleship.* Lexington, KY: Owl's Nest, 2014.

Putman, David. *Breaking the Discipleship Code: Becoming a Missional Follower of Jesus.* Nashville, TN: B&H Publishing Group, 2008.

Putman, Jim. *Real-Life Discipleship: Building Churches: Building That Make Disciples.* Colorado Springs, CO: NavPress, 2010.

Putman, Jim, and Bobby Harrington. *DiscipleShift: Five Steps That Help Your Church to Make Disciples Who Make Disciples.* Grand Rapids, MI: Zondervan, 2013.

Roberts Jr., Bob. *Transformation: Discipleship that Turns Lives, Churches, and the World Upside Down.* Grand Rapids, MI: Zondervan, 2006.

Self, Charlie. *Flourishing Churches and Communities: A Pentecostal Primer on Faith, Work, and Economics for Spirit-Empowered Discipleship.* Grand Rapids, MI: Christian's Library Press, 2013.

Watson, David L. and Paul D. Watson. *Contagious Disciple Making: Leading Others on a Journey of Discovery.* Nashville, TN: Thomas Nelson, 2014.

White, James Emery. *Rethinking the Church: A Challenge to Creative Redesign in an Age of Transition.* Grand Rapids, MI: Baker Books, 2006.

Wilkins, Michael J. *Following the Master: A Biblical Theology of Discipleship.* Grand Rapids, MI: Zondervan, 1992.

About the Author

Stan Cook is a husband, father, and proud Papa. He is also a pastor, author, speaker, and teacher. He is an ordained minister in the Assemblies of God and has over thirty years of practical ministry as a high school Bible teacher, youth pastor, Christian education pastor, worship leader, interim pastor, bi-vocational pastor, and lead pastor.

Stan and his wife, Heidi, live in Louisville, Kentucky. They have four adult children and three grandchildren.

Stan has earned a Master of Arts in Ministerial Leadership from Southeastern University in Lakeland, Florida, and a Doctor of Ministry from The Assemblies of God Theological Seminary in Springfield, Missouri.

He enjoys reading, playing basketball and golf, and spending time with his wonderful grandchildren.

Endnotes

Introduction

1. Greg Ogden, *Discipleship Essentials: A Guide to Building Your Life in Christ* (Downers Grove, IL: InterVarsity Press, 2007), 20.

2. M. Eugene Boring, New Testament Articles, Matthew, Mark, vol. 8 of New Interpreter's Bible: A Commentary in Twelve Volumes (Nashville, TN: Abingdon Press, 1995), 503.

3. Eugene Peterson, A Long Obedience in the Same Direction: Discipleship in an Instant Society (Downers Grove, IL: InterVarsity Press, 2000), 17.

4. All Scripture quotations, unless otherwise noted, are from the English Standard Version.

5. Greg Ogden, Transforming Discipleship: Making Disciples a Few at a Time (Downers Grove, IL: InterVarsity Press, 2003), 17.

6. For a list of the thirty-five outcomes and five domains, see: "Psychometrics: The Science Behind the Assessment," Discipleship Dynamics, accessed July 14, 2021, https://discipleshipdynamics.com/psychometrics/.

7. Paul Tanner, "The Cost of Discipleship: Losing One's life for Jesus' Sake," Journal of Evangelical Theological Society 56, no. 1 (2013): 61.

PART ONE

8. M. Rex Miller, *The Millennium Matrix: Reclaiming the Past, Reframing the Future of the Church* (San Francisco, CA: Jossey-Bass, 2004), 159.

9. Charlie Self, *Flourishing Churches and Communities: A Pentecostal Primer on Faith, Work, and Economics for Spirit-Empowered Discipleship* (Grand Rapids, MI: Christians

Library Press, 2013), 11.

10. Michael J. Wilkins, *Following the Master: A Biblical Theology of Discipleship* (Grand Rapids, MI: Zondervan, 1992), 39.

11. Ibid.

12. All Scripture quotations, unless otherwise noted, are from the English Standard Version.

13. Dan Nässelqvist, "Disciple" in *The Lexham Bible Dictionary*, eds. James Barry, et al. (Bellingham, WA: Lexham Press, 2016), Logos Bible Software.

14. Andrew Dragos, "7 Things the Bible Teaches about Discipleship," Seedbed, January 29, 2018, accessed March 24, 2019, http://www.seedbed.com/7-things-the-Bible-teaches-about-discipleship/.

Chapter 1: The Biblical Mandate for Discipleship: The Great Commission

15. Timothy Tennent, *Invitation to World Missions: A Trinitarian Missiology for the Twenty-first Century* (Grand Rapids, MI: Kregel, 2010), 127.

16. Ibid. "The Gospel of Matthew does not specifically use such a term. In fact, the phrase 'Great Commission' does not appear until late in Christian history. Some scholars argue that it was coined by Baron Justinian von Welz, a 17th-century Lutheran nobleman, who argued that the words in Matthew 28 meant that all Christians were required to spread the faith, not just Jesus' closest disciples." Matthew Schmalz, "What is the Great Commission and Why is it so Controversial?," The Conversation, February 8, 2019, accessed March 16, 2019, http://theconversation.com/what-is-the-great-commission-and-why-is-it-so-controversial-111138.

17. Craig Keener, "Matthew's Missiology: Making Disciples of the Nations (Matthew 28:19-20)," *Asian Journal of*

Pentecostal Studies, 12:1 (2009): 19.

18. R. T. France, *Matthew: An Introduction and Commentary,* vol. 1 of, *Tyndale New Testament Commentaries* (Downers Grove, IL: InterVarsity Press, 1985), 419, Logos Bible Software.

19. R. T. France, *The Gospel of Matthew,* The New International Commentary on the New Testament (Grand Rapids, MI: Wm. B. Eerdmans Publication Co., 2007), 1112–1113, Logos Bible Software. France notes, "'All authority in heaven and on earth has been given to me' echoes Dan 7:14, 'To him was given dominion and glory and kingship, that all peoples, nations and languages should serve him,' a kingship which is to be everlasting and indestructible; there will be further echoes of Dan 7:14 in the mission to 'all the nations,' v. 19, and in Jesus' powerful presence until 'the end of the age,' v. 20. Jesus has spoken several times, using the language of Dan 7:13–14, of the future sovereignty of the Son of Man (16:28; 19:28; 24:30–31; 25:31–34; 26:64); three of those passages have indicated that that sovereignty would be achieved in the near future, to be seen by those then alive (16:28; 24:30–34; 26:64; cf. also 10:23). But now what has been a vision for the future, albeit the imminent future, has become present reality. The risen Jesus, vindicated over those who tried to destroy him, is now established as the universal sovereign, and his realm embraces not only the whole earth which was to be the dominion of the 'one like a son of man' in Daniel's vision but heaven as well."

20. Craig Blomberg, *Matthew,* vol. 22 of The New American Commentary (Nashville: Broadman & Holman Publishers, 1992), 431, Logos Bible Software.

21. David Turner and Darrell L. Bock, *Matthew and Mark,* vol. 11 of Cornerstone Biblical Commentary (Carol Stream, IL: Tyndale House Publishers, 2005), 375, Logos Bible Software.

22. Michael J. Wilkins, *Matthew*, The NIV Application Commentary (Grand Rapids, MI: Zondervan Publishing House, 2004), 953, Logos Bible Software. Wilkins posits: "The object of making disciples is 'all the nations.' People of every nation are to receive the opportunity to become Jesus' disciples. When we read the Commission here in the light of Luke's Gospel, that 'repentance and forgiveness of sins … be preached in his name to all nations, beginning at Jerusalem' (Luke 24:47), we understand that Jesus' ministry in Israel was the beginning point of a universal offer of salvation to all the peoples of the earth."

23. Wilkins, *Matthew*, 951. Keener concurs: "Jesus' closing words in Matthew's Gospel include one imperative surrounded by three subordinate participial clauses, which is to say, one command that is carried out in three ways. The command is implement-ted by going, baptizing, and teaching." Keener, "Matthew's Missiology," 3.

24. Wilkins, *Matthew*, 952.

25. Blomberg, *Matthew*, 431. Blomberg notes, "The main command of Christ's commission is 'make disciples' (*mathēteusate*). Too much and too little have often been made of this observation. Too much is made of it when the disciples' 'going' is overly subordinated, so that Jesus' charge is to proselytize merely where one is. Matthew frequently uses 'go' as an introductory circumstantial participle that is rightly translated as coordinate to the main verb—here 'Go and make' (cf. 2:8; 9:13; 11:4; 17:27; 28:7). Too little is made of it when all attention is centered on the command to 'go,' as in countless appeals for missionary candidates, so that foreign missions are elevated to a higher status of Christian service than other forms of spiritual activity."

26. Roger L. Hahn, *Matthew: A Biblical Commentary in the*

Wesleyan Tradition (Indianapolis, IN: Wesleyan Publishing House, 2007), 346, Logos Bible Software.

27. Nässelqvist, "Disciple."

28. Wilkins, *Following the Master,* 93. Wilkins notes, "Second, on the surface Jesus' disciples appeared to be similar to other forms of Jewish disciples, Some of Jesus' own disciples quite likely followed him in a mistaken fashion, expecting Jesus to be like other revolutionary leaders and their disciples."

29. Paul Helm, "Disciple," in *Baker Encyclopedia of the Bible*, ed. Walter A. Elwell (Grand Rapids, MI: Baker Book House, 1988), 629, Logos Bible Software.

30. Hans Kvalbein, "Go Therefore and Make Disciples ... The Concept of Discipleship in the New Testament," *Themelios* 13, no. 2 (February 1988), 18.

31. Wilkins, *Following the Master*, 93

32. Ibid.

33. Michael J. Wilkins, "Discipleship," in *Dictionary of Jesus and the Gospels,* ed. Joel B. and Scot McKnight Green (Downers Grove, IL: InterVarsity Press, 1992), 182, Logos Bible Software.

34. Paul Tanner, "The Cost of Discipleship: Losing One's Life for Jesus' Sake," *Journal of the Evangelical Theological Society* 56, no. 1 (2013): 46.

35. Robert E. Webber, *Ancient-Future Evangelism: Making Your Church a Faith-Forming Community* (Grand Rapids, MI: Baker Books, 2003), 22.

36. Chris Shirley, "It Takes a Church to Make a Disciple: An Integrative Model of Discipleship for the Local Church," *Southwestern Journal of Theology* 50, no. 2 (Spring 2008): 209.

37. Kvalbein, "Go Therefore and Make," 40. Kvalbein notes,

"The relationship of Jesus to his disciples was different. Jesus had a unique position that could not be transferred to his disciples."

38. Robby Gallaty, *Growing Up: How to Be a Disciple Who Makes Disciples* (Nashville, TN: B&H Publishing Group, 2013), xxv.

39. Greg Ogden, *Transforming Discipleship: Making Disciples a Few at a Time* (Downers Grove, IL: InterVarsity Press, 2003), 42.

40. Opoku Onyinah, "The Meaning of Discipleship," *International Review of Mission* 106, no. 2 (December 2017): 222.

41. Russell L. Huizing, "Leaders from Disciples: The Church's Contribution to Leadership Development," *Evangelical Review of Theology* 35, no. 4 (2011): 334. Eddie Gibbs similarly notes that "Jesus' disciples were commanded to share what they themselves had learned through experience, command and commentary. They were to teach in the same way that they themselves had been taught—by the apprenticeship method. In other words, they were to draw others into the orbit of their own experience." Eddie Gibbs, *ChurchNext: Quantum Changes in How We do Ministry* (Downers Grove, IL: InterVarsity Press, 2000), 56.

42. Jim Putman, *Real-Life Discipleship: Building Churches that Make Disciples* (Colorado Springs, CO: NavPress, 2010), 35.

43. James A. Lilly, *Great Commission Disciple Making: Growing Disciples Rooted in God's Word* (Maitland, FL: Xulon Press, 2016), 4.

44. Leland Ryken, et al., eds, "Disciple, Discipleship" in *Dictionary of Biblical Imagery* (Downers Grove, IL: InterVarsity Press, 2000), Logos Bible Software.

45. Bill Hull, *Jesus Christ Disciplemaker* (Grand Rapids, MI: Baker Books, 2007), 14-15.

46. Ibid., 15.

47. Ibid., 15-22.

48. Lilly, *Great Commission Disciple Making*, 4.

49. France, *The Gospel of Matthew*, 145.

50. Sylvia Wilkey Collinson, *Making Disciples: The Significance of Jesus' Educational Methods for Today's Church* (Eugene, OR: Wipf and Stock Publishers, 2006), 98-99.

51. Ibid.

52. Blomberg, *Matthew*, 90-91. France notes, "*Follow me* (literally 'come behind me') would immediately suggest the disciples of a Rabbi (see Davies, pp. 422-423), who literally followed him around to absorb his teaching, though this was by their own choice, not by his summons. A good teacher would be expected to have a group of such 'followers.' But Jesus calls his disciples not only to listen and learn, but to take an active part as *fishers of men*. Jeremiah 16:16 had spoken of fishing for men, but this was to catch them for judgment (cf. Amos 4:2); Jesus' 'fishermen' will save men from judgment." France, *The Gospel of Matthew*, 109.

53. Nässelqvist, "Disciple."

54. Ibid.

55. Ibid.

56. Donald A. Hagner, *Matthew 1-13,* vol. 33A of *Word Biblical Commentary* (Nashville, TN: Thomas Nelson, 1993), 78, Logos Bible Software.

57. William Barclay, *Gospel of Matthew,* vol. 1 of *The New Daily Study Bible* (Louisville, KY: Westminster John Knox Press, 2001), 90.

58. Bill Hull, *Conversion and Discipleship: You Can't Have One without the Other* (Grand Rapids, MI: Zondervan, 2016), 175.

59. Putman, *Real-Life,* 29.

60. Ibid., 29-30.

61. Wilkins, *Following the Master,* 357.

62. Onyinah, "The Meaning of Discipleship," 221.

63. Keener notes, "If God called shepherds like Moses and David to shepherd his people Israel, Jesus could call fishermen to be gatherers of people. Some great men and women of God in the Bible never even became public expositors of Scripture; aside from his prophetic gifts, Joseph's witness involved especially public administration, learned in Potiphar's house and a prison and then applied to all Egypt." Craig S. Keener, *Matthew,* vol. 1 of *The IVP New Testament Commentary Series* (Downers Grove, IL: InterVarsity Press, 1997), Matthew 4:19, Logos Bible Software.

64. Bill Hull, *The Complete Book of Discipleship: On Being and Making Followers of Christ* (Colorado Springs, CO: NavPress, 2006), 177.

65. William L. Lane, *The Gospel of Mark,* The New International Commentary on the New Testament (Grand Rapids, MI: Wm. B. Eerdmans Publishing Company, 1974), 69, Logos Bible Software.

66. Hahn, *Matthew*, 78.

67. Doug Redford, *The Life and Ministry of Jesus: The Gospels,* vol. 1 of *Standard Reference Library: New Testament* (Cincinnati, OH: Standard Publishing, 2007), 123, Logos Bible Software.

68. Wilkins, "Discipleship," 186.

69. Wilkins, *Matthew*, 177. Barclay Newman and Phillip Stine add clarity to this implication: "The adverb *Immediately* is in focus here as it is in verse 22. It represents a form of the adverb which is favored by Matthew, who uses it twelve times (see 8:3; 13:5; 14:22, 31; 20:34; 24:29; 25:16; 26:49, 74; 27:48), as compared to six times by Luke, three times by John, and

none by Mark. It should be translated 'At once,' 'Right away,' or 'Without delay.' *They left their nets*, that is, 'they left their nets right there,' 'they abandoned their nets,' or 'they quit working with their nets.'" Barclay M. Newman and Phillip C. Stine, *A Handbook on the Gospel of Matthew* (New York, NY: United Bible Societies, 1988), 96, Logos Bible Software.

70. Ulrich Luz, *Matthew 1-7*, Hermeneia—A Critical and Historical Commentary on the Bible (Minneapolis, MN: Fortress Press, 2007), 162, Logos Bible Software.

71. Hagner, *Matthew 1-13*, 77.

72. Ibid.

73. Huizing, "Leaders from Disciples," 334.

74. Webber, *Ancient-Future Evangelism*, 22. Webber notes, "The Great Commission demonstrates that Jesus did not introduce various programs for evangelism, discipleship, and Christian formation. Instead, following the tradition of Hebraic holism, Jesus taught that becoming a disciple is a process that takes place in a continuous way in the worship and community life of the church."

75. Hull, *The Complete Book of Discipleship*, 28-29.

Chapter 2: Discipleship in the Old Testament

76. James G. Samra, "A Biblical View of Discipleship," *Bibliotheca Sacra* 160 (2003), 226.

77. Marcel V. Macelaru, "Discipleship in the Old Testament and Its Context: A Phenomenological Approach," *Pleroma anul XIII* 2 (2011), 15.

78. Dragos, "7 Things the Bible Teaches."

79. Helm, "Disciple," 629.

80. Ryken, "Disciple, Discipleship."

81. David R Bauer, "Disciple, Discipleship," in *New Interpreter's Dictionary of the Bible: D-H,* vol. 2, ed. Katherine Doob

Sakenfeld (Nashville, TN: Abingdon Press, 2007), 128.

82. Wilkins, *Following the Master*, 52-53.

83. Macelaru, "Discipleship in the Old Testament," 18-20.

84. Ibid., 20.

85. Ibid., 19.

86. Samra, "A Biblical View of Discipleship," 226.

87. Wilkins, *Following the Master*, 64.

88. Stephen Szikszai, "Elisha," in *Interpreter's Dictionary of the Bible: E-J,* vol. 2, ed. George Arthur Buttrick (Nashville, TN: Abingdon Press, 1962), 91.

89. Ibid.

90. Duane Garrett notes, "The author is called 'the Teacher [Qoheleth], son of David, king in Jerusalem.' This verse, in conjunction with v. 12, implies Solomonic authorship. The precise meaning of Qoheleth (here rendered 'the Teacher') is uncertain. The word may mean a 'speaker in the assembly.' The verse indicates that although the author of the work is Solomon, he writes under the role-name 'the Teacher.' He is not speaking in the capacity of a king but as a teacher. The book contains advice and reflection rather than decrees." Duane A. Garrett, *Proverbs, Ecclesiastes, Song of Songs,* vol. 14 of *The New American Commentary* (Nashville, TN: Broadman & Holman Publishers, 1993), 282, Logos Bible Software.

91. Leslie C. Allen, *Jeremiah: A Commentary*, The Old Testament Library (Louisville, KY: Westminster John Knox Press, 2008), 397, Logos Bible Software.

92. Wilkins, *Following the Master,* 56-57.

Chapter 3: Discipleship in the New Testament

93. Helm, "Disciple," 630.

94. Wilkins, *Following the Master,* 52-53.

95. Michael J. Wilkins, "Peter's Theology of Discipleship to the Crucified Messiah (1 Peter 2:18-25)," *Southern Baptist Journal of Theology* 21, no. 3 (2017): 61.

96. Ibid.

97. Ibid., 61-62.

98. Webber, *Ancient-Future Evangelism,* 73.

99. Ibid.

100. Gibbs, *ChurchNext,* 56.

101. Onyinah, "The Meaning of Discipleship," 219.

102. Webber, *Ancient-Future Evangelism,* 142.

103. Kvalbein, "Go Therefore and Make Disciples," 39.

104. Wilkins, "Peter's Theology of Discipleship," 58-59.

105. Ibid., 61.

106. Collinson, *Making Disciples*, 98.

107. John R. Higgins, Michael L. Dusing, and Frank D. Tallman, *An Introduction to Theology: A Classical Pentecostal Perspective* (Dubuque, IO: Kendall/Hunt Publishing Company, 1994), 167.

108. Shirley, "It Takes a Church to Make a Disciple," 209.

109. Terence L. Donaldson, "Guiding Readers—Making Disciples: Discipleship in Matthew's Narrative Strategy" in *Patterns of Discipleship in the New Testament*, ed. Richard N. Longenecker (Grand Rapids, MI: Wm. B. Eerdmans Publishing Company, 1996), 33.

110. David Putman, *Breaking the Discipleship Code: Becoming a Missional Follower of Jesus* (Nashville, TN: B&H Publishing Group, 2008), 34.

111. Ibid.

112. Higgins, *An Introduction to Theology, 175.*

113. Ross Rohde, *Viral Jesus: Recovering the Contagious Power of the Gospel* (Lake Mary, FL: Passio, 2012), 90.

114. Hull, *Conversion and Discipleship*, 178.

115. Ibid.

116. Bill Hull, *The Disciple-Making Church: Leading a Body of Believers on the Journey of Faith* (Grand Rapids, MI: Baker Books, 2010), 68.

117. Kvalbein, "Go Therefore and Make Disciples," 39.

118. Charles A. Davis, *Making Disciples Across Cultures: Missional Principles for a Diverse World* (Downers Grove, IL: IVP Books, 2015), 36.

119. Shirley, "It Takes a Church," 211.

120. Ibid.

121. Ron Bennett explores 2 Timothy 2:2, noting, "In 2 Timothy 2:2, the apostle Paul shows how life-to-life relationships work in three directions. Paul mentored Timothy, and Timothy in turn mentored others. In addition, Timothy connected with 'many witnesses'—evidently peers on the same spiritual journey—for sources of mutual encouragement, accountability and protection." Ron Bennett, *Intentional Disciplemaking: Cultivating Spiritual Maturity in the Local Church* (Colorado Springs, CO: NavPress, 2001), 31.

122. Wilkins, "Peter's Theology of Discipleship," 53.

123. Bob McNabb, *Spiritual Multiplication in the Real World: Why Some Disciple-makers Reproduce When Others Fail* (n.p.: Multiplication Press, 2013), 44.

124. Wilkins, *Following the Master*, 25-34.

125. Lee C. Camp, *Mere Discipleship: Radical Christianity in a Rebellious World* (Grand Rapids, MI: Brazos Press, 2008), 209.

PART TWO

126. Mike Breen and the 3DM Team, *Building a Discipling Culture: How to Release a Missional Movement by Discipling People Like Jesus Did* (n.p.: 3DM Publishing, 2011), 20.

Chapter 4: The Heart of Discipleship

127. Beverly Vos, "The Spiritual Disciplines and Christian Ministry," *Evangelical Review of Theology* 36, no. 2 (2012): 101.

128. Opoku Onyinah, "The Meaning of Discipleship," *International Review of Mission* 106, no. 2 (December 2017): 221.

129. Robert E. Logan and Charles R. Ridley, *The Discipleship Difference: Making Disciples While Growing as Disciples* (San Bernardino, CA: Logan Leadership, 2016), 83.

130. Ibid.

131. Breen, *Building a Discipling Culture*, 38.

132. Russell L. Huizing, "Leaders from Disciples: The Church's Contribution to Leadership Development," *Evangelical Review of Theology* 35, no. 4 (2011): 334.

133. Ibid.

134. Michael J. Wilkins, "Peter's Theology of Discipleship to the Crucified Messiah (1 Peter 2:18-25)," *Southern Baptist Journal of Theology* 21, no. 3 (2017): 62.

135. Bobby Harrington and Alex Absalom, *Discipleship that Fits: The Five Kinds of Relationships God Uses to Help Us Grow* (Grand Rapids, MI: Zondervan, 2016), 16. The authors further note, "What we want you to see is that being a disciple is all about becoming like Jesus, and then helping others become like Jesus, because that is the way God has designed for us to experience fullness of life."

136. Edward N. Gross, *Are You a Christian or a Disciple?*

Rediscovering & Renewing New Testament Discipleship (Maitland, FL: Xulon Press, 2014), 26.

137. Ibid.

138. David L. Watson and Paul D. Watson, *Contagious Disciple Making: Leading Others on a Journey of Discovery* (Nashville, TN: Thomas Nelson, 2014), 205.

139. Bill Hull, *Choose the Life: Exploring a Faith That Embraces Discipleship* (Grand Rapids, MI: Baker Books, 2004), 11.

140. Eric Geiger, Michael Kelley, and Philip Nation, *Transformational Discipleship: How People Really Grow* (Nashville, TN: B&H Publishing Group, 2012), 11.

141. Breen, *Building a Discipling Culture,* 11.

142. Ibid.

143. Paul Tanner, "The Cost of Discipleship: Losing One's Life for Jesus' Sake," *Journal of Evangelical Theological Society* 56, no. 1 (2013): 61.

144. Ibid.

145. Bobby Harrington and Josh Patrick, *The Disciple Maker's Handbook: 7 Elements of a Discipleship Lifestyle* (Grand Rapids, MI: Zondervan, 2017), 92.

Chapter 5: Disciple-Making in Church Practice

146. Greg Ogden, *Transforming Discipleship: Making Disciples a Few at a Time* (Downers Grove, IL: InterVarsity Press, 2003), 17. Ogden posits that three critical issues must be addressed in any disciple-making strategy: (1) disciple-making is about relational investment, (2) we rightly associate disciple-making with multiplication, and (3) making disciples is a transformative process.

147. Jim Putman and Bobby Harrington, *DiscipleShift: Five Steps that Help Your Church to Make Disciples Who Make Disciples* (Grand Rapids, MI: Zondervan, 2013), 21.

148. Ron Bennett, *Intentional Disciplemaking: Cultivating Spiritual Maturity in the Local Church* (Colorado Springs, CO: NavPress, 2001), 24.

149. Ibid., 35.

150. Ibid., 37. Bennett notes, "The reality of life in God's kingdom must center on transformation, not conformation. In Colossians 1, Paul explains this dramatic change as a transfer from the kingdom of darkness to the kingdom of light. To be sure, life in the kingdom of light is unlike anything we have ever known. But being transferred from darkness to light only marks the beginning of the transforming reality of discipleship."

151. Onyinah, "The Meaning of Discipleship," 219.

152. James Emery White, *Rethinking the Church: A Challenge to Creative Redesign in an Age of Transition* (Grand Rapids, MI: Baker Books, 2006), 67.

153. Geiger, Kelley, and Nation, *Transformational Discipleship*, 8.

154. Ibid., 10. The authors further note that "Discipleship is a word that is often hijacked and haphazardly tossed around to describe a multitude of things. And because it has become such a nebulous term, people launch complaints about a ministry described as 'discipleship' that may not have the slightest resemblance to what is possible in delivering transformation to people," Ibid., 17.

155. Ogden, *Transforming Discipleship*, 15.

156. Ibid.

157. Ibid.

158. Ibid.

159. Ibid.

160. Ibid.

161. Mark Dever, *Discipling: How to Help Others Follow Jesus* (Wheaton, IL: Crossway, 2016), 14.

162. Onyinah, "The Meaning of Discipleship," 221.

163. Ibid.

164. Julia Duin, *Quitting Church: Why the Faithful are Fleeing and What to do About it* (Grand Rapids, MI: Baker Books, 2008), 50.

165. Watson and Watson, *Contagious Disciple Making*, 204.

166. Ibid.

167. Onyinah, "The Meaning of Discipleship," 222.

168. Ibid.

169. Robby Gallaty, *Growing Up: How to Be a Disciple Who Makes Disciples* (Nashville, TN: B&H Publishing Group, 2013), 25.

170. Breen, *Building a Discipling Culture*, 18. Breen notes that "A gifted discipler is someone who invites people into a covenantal relationship with him or her, but challenges that person to live into his or her true identity in very direct and graceful ways. Without both dynamics working together, you will not see people grow into the people God has created them to be."

171. Logan and Ridley, *The Discipleship Difference*, 98.

172. Ibid., 98.

173. Ibid., 98.

174. Ibid., 99.

175. Ibid., 102.

176. Ibid., 103.

177. Ibid., 104.

178. Robert E. Webber, *Ancient-Future Evangelism: Making Your Church a Faith-Forming Community* (Grand Rapids, MI: Baker Books, 2004), 24. Webber continues, "Initial

conversion brought the seeker into the church. Here the new believer spent considerable time as a hearer, learning how to live the Christian life. Next, the hearer moved to the stage of kneeler where he or she was instructed more deeply into the faith of the church, into the life of prayer, and into the reality of spiritual warfare. At the end of this period the believer was baptized into full membership in the church. Finally, in this state of belonging, the believer was known as faithful. In this fourth stage of spiritual formation, he or she learned more about the mystery of worship, especially a fuller meaning of baptism and the Eucharistic meal."

179. Wilkins, "Peter's Theology of Discipleship," 69-70.

180. Craig Van Gelder, *The Essence of the Church: A Community Created by the Spirit* (Grand Rapids, MI: Baker Books, 2000), 152.

181. Logan and Ridley, *Discipleship Difference*, 153.

182. Bennett, *Intentional Disciplemaking*, 25.

183. Ibid.

184. John F. O'Grady, *Disciples and Leaders: The Origins of Christian Ministry in the New Testament* (Mehwah, NJ: Paulist Press, 1991), 5.

185. Ibid.

186. Hans Kvalbein, "Go Therefore and Make Disciples … The Concept of Discipleship in the New Testament," *Themelios* 13, no. 2 (February 1998), 49.

187. Aubrey Malphurs, *Strategic Disciplemaking: A Practical Tool for Successful Ministry* (Grand Rapids, MI: Baker Books, 2009), 19.

188. Greg Ogden, *Discipleship Essentials: A Guide to Building Your Life in Christ* (Downers Grove, IL: InterVarsity Press, 2007), 21.

189. Logan and Ridley, *The Discipleship Difference*, 11.

190. James A. Lilly, *Great Commission Disciple Making: Growing Disciples Rooted in God's Word* (Maitland, FL: Xulon Press, 2016), 10.

191. Vos, "The Spiritual Disciplines and Christian Ministry," 100.

192. Ogden, *Discipleship Essentials*, 21.

193. Watson and Watson, *Contagious Disciple Making,* 204. The authors note that "In the modern church, discipleship is an educational process designed to orient new believers to the biblical and historical practices of our churches. Even in some extremely Bible-oriented materials, the emphasis is on knowing God's Word, with some admonition to obey, but without the relationship necessary to see it happen. There is a misconception that if people know what is right, they will do what is right."

194. Bob Roberts, Jr., *Transformation: Discipleship that Turns Lives, Churches, and the World Upside Down* (Grand Rapids, MI: Zondervan, 2006), 69.

195. Watson and Watson, *Contagious Disciple Making*, 204.

196. Dave Early and Rod Dempsey, *Disciple Making Is... How to Live in the Great Commission with Passion and Confidence* (Nashville, TN: B&H Publishing Group, 2013), 51.

197. Roberts, *Transformation*, 69.

198. Larry Osborne, *Mission Creep: The 5 Subtle Shifts that Sabotage Evangelism & Discipleship* (Lexington, KY: Owl's Nest, 2014), 47.

199. Harrington and Patrick, *The Disciple Maker's Handbook*, 77.

200. Breen, *Building a Discipling Culture*, 28.

201. Logan and Ridley, *The Discipleship Difference*, 25.

202. Breen, *Building a Discipling Culture*, 28.

203. Onyinah, "The Meaning of Discipleship," 220.

204. Robby Gallaty, *Rediscovering Discipleship: Making Jesus' Final Words Our First Work* (Grand Rapids, MI: Zondervan, 2015), 87.

205. Edward H. Hammett, *Reframing Spiritual Formation: Discipleship in an Unchurched Culture* (Macon, GA: Smith & Helwys Publishing Incorporated, 2002), 101.

206. Ogden, *Transforming Discipleship*, 43.

207. Ibid.

208. Bill Hull, *The Complete Book of Discipleship: On Being and Making Followers of Christ* (Colorado Springs, CO: NavPress, 2006), 67-68.

209. Ray S. Anderson, *An Emergent Theology for Emerging Churches* (Downers Grove, IL: IVP Books, 2006), 115. Anderson writes, "Too often, I fear, … the church attempts to make disciples out of Christians by urging them to follow Christ. What is really intended is to mobilize the members of the church to take up church-related ministries and to develop their own interior life."

210. Bennett, *Intentional Disciplemaking*, 24.

211. Ogden, *Transforming Discipleship*, 43.

212. Huizing, "Leaders from Disciples," 338.

213. M. Robert Mulholland, *The Deeper Journey: The Spirituality of Discovering Your True Self* (Downers Grove, IL: InterVarsity Press, 2006), 69.

214. Diane J. Chandler, *Christian Spiritual Formation: An Integrated Approach for Personal and Relational Wholeness* (Downers Grove, IL: IVP Academic, 2014), 19.

215. Ray S. Anderson, *On Being Human: Essays in Theological Anthropology* (Eugene, OR: Wipf and Stock Publishers, 2010), 86. On the *imago Dei,* Anderson writes, "Human persons are not identical with the *imago,* but bear the *imago*

in the form of the human itself (the *humanum* which each person bears). This *imago* endowment, which causes the creaturely being that we call a human person to exist, is not a subsequent endowment on an already-existing human-like being. Because the *imago* is borne by the human person in the form of the human itself (*humanum*), there is continuity of the *imago*, even through the fall and as a sinner."

216. Bill Clem, *Disciple: Getting Your Identity from Jesus* (Wheaton, IL: Crossway, 2011), 72.

217. Michael J. Wilkins, *Following the Master: A Biblical Theology of Discipleship* (Grand Rapids, MI: Zondervan, 1992), 42.

218. Charlie Self, *Flourishing Churches and Communities: A Pentecostal Primer on Faith, Work, and Economics for Spirit-Empowered Discipleship* (Grand Rapids, MI: Christian's Library Press, 2013), 15.

219. Michael J. Wilkins, "Disciple, Discipleship" in *Baker's Evangelical Dictionary of Theology*, ed. Walter A. Elwell (Grand Rapids, MI: Baker Books, 1997), 175.

220. Onyinah, "The Meaning of Discipleship," 222.

221. Steven M. Fettke, "Pentecostal Spiritual Formation for the 21st Century" (transcript for a presentation for the Society for Pentecostal Studies 44th Annual Meeting, Lakeland, FL, 2015), http://sps-usa.org/store/products. Fettke notes, "In living the life of a disciple, believers can begin to realize that God wishes to purge us of our need to control, our agendas, our false selves and others. God wants believers to be in union with God. From that union will come all that is needed to live out a loving, sanctified life."

222. Anderson, *On Being Human*, 63.

223. Anderson, *An Emergent Theology for Emerging Churches*, 142.

224. Marcel V. Macelaru, "Discipleship in the Old Testament and Its Context: A Phenomenological Approach," *Pleroma* 13, no. 2 (2011): 13.

225. Logan and Ridley, *The Discipleship Difference*, 77.

226. Gabe Lyons, *The Next Christians: The Good News About the End of Christian America* (New York: Doubleday Religion, 2010), 151. Lyons notes, "There's something special about communities that can soothe the brokenness in our personal lives. If you could think about it, God could easily heal our ills and solve our problems. At the very least, he might eliminate them altogether from the lives of his most devout followers. But, apparently, that's not his way. Instead, we need the support of others inside the context of a Christian community."

227. Gallaty, *Growing Up*, xix.

228. Onyinah, "The Meaning of Discipleship," 226.

229. George Barna and Greg Kinnaman, *Churchless: Understanding Today's Unchurched and How to Connect with Them* (Carol Stream, IL: Tyndale Momentum, 2014), 4.

230. Hammett, *Reframing Spiritual Formation*, 100.

231. Bennett, *Intentional Disciplemaking*, 50. Bennett writes, "A loving, disciplemaking church maximizes effectiveness by learning more about how non-Christians think and feel. This type of church also recognizes that three broad categories of non-Christians exist: the lost within the church, the lost who will visit the church, and the lost who will not visit the church. This awareness enables more effective outreach."

232. Ibid., 48.

233. Ralph Moore, *Making Disciples: Developing Lifelong Followers of Jesus* (Venture, CA: Regal Books, 2012), 115.

234. Charles A. Davis, *Making Disciples Across Cultures: Missional Principles for a Diverse World* (Downers Grove, IL:

IVP Books, 2015), 35-36. Davis adds, "The learning process of becoming a disciple begins long before one understands enough to proclaim him as Lord and continues until we come face-to-face with him and know him as he knows us. Peter and the other apostles were learning of Jesus for well over a year before the spiritual light pierced through the darkness to their hearts and Peter proclaimed Jesus as 'the Christ, the Son of the living God' (Mt 16:16)."

235. Gene Edward Veith, Jr., *God at Work: Your Christian Vocation in All of Life* (Wheaton, IL: Crossway, 2002), 17.

236. Tom Nelson, *Work Matters: Connecting Sunday Worship to Monday Work* (Wheaton, IL: Crossway, 2011), 16. Nelson writes, "The word *vocation* simply means 'calling.' Properly understood, Christian vocation is centered in a sovereign God who calls us to embrace the gospel of Jesus Christ and to follow him in the power of the Holy Spirit as his disciples."

237. Steven Garber, *Visions of Vocation: Common Grace for the Common Good* (Downers Grove, IL: IVP Books, 2014), 11.

238. Ibid.

239. Discipleship Dynamics LLC, "The Assessment in Detail," Discipleship Dynamics, 2016, accessed February 7, 2018, https://discipleshipdynamics.com/about-the-assessment/.

240. Ibid.

241. Ibid.

242. Nelson, *Work Matters*, 77.

243. Wilkins, "Peter's Theology of Discipleship," 59.

Chapter 6: Whole-Life Disciple-Making Exemplified in Two Dimensions

244. As a reminder: when I first became aware of the Discipleship Dynamics tool to help promote whole-life disciples while

doing my doctoral studies, I learned about the *thirty-five biblical discipleship outcomes* and *five domains* (see https://discipleshipdynamics.com/psychometrics/ for a listing of both) of a holistic approach to discipleship: Spiritual Foundations, Personal Wholeness, Healthy Relationships, Vocational Clarity, and Economics and Work. The scope of this present book will address *only the first two* of the five dimensions/domains of Discipleship Dynamics: Spiritual Formation and Personal Wholeness.

245. Keith J. Vanhoozer, "Putting on Christ: Spiritual Formation and the Drama of Discipleship," *Journal of Spiritual Formation & Soul Care* 8, no. 2 (2015): 147-148.

246. Discipleship Dynamics LLC, "The Assessment in Detail."

247. Ibid.

248. Hull, *The Complete Book of Discipleship*, 19.

249. Keith Meyer, "Whole-Life Transformation" in *The Kingdom Life: A Practical Theology of Discipleship and Spiritual Formation,* ed. Alan Andrews (Colorado Springs, CO: NavPress, 2010), 139.

250. Discipleship Dynamics LLC, "The Assessment in Detail."

251. Fettke, "Spiritual Formation in the 21st Century," 6.

252. Discipleship Dynamics LLC, "The Assessment in Detail."

253. Ibid.

254. Lilly, *Great Commission Disciple Making*, 13.

255. Discipleship Dynamics LLC, "The Assessment in Detail."

256. Ibid.

257. Ibid.

258. Ibid.

259. Richard J. Foster, *Celebration of Discipline: The Path to Spiritual Growth* (San Francisco, CA: HarperSanFrancisco, 1998), 18.

260. Discipleship Dynamics LLC, "The Assessment in Detail."

261. Hull, *The Complete Book of Discipleship*, 129.

262. Discipleship Dynamics LLC, "The Assessment in Detail."

263. Terry A. Bowland, *Make Disciples: Reaching the Postmodern World for Christ* (Joplin, MO: College Press Publishing Company, 2005), 157-164.

264. Ibid., 34.

265. Discipleship Dynamics LLC, "The Assessment in Detail."

266. Stephen A. Macchia, *Becoming a Healthy Disciple: 10 Traits of a Vital Christian* (Lexington, MA: Leadership Transformations, 2013), 96.

267. Discipleship Dynamics LLC, "The Assessment in Detail."

268. Ibid.

269. Ruth Haley Barton, *Strengthening the Soul of Your Leadership: Seeking God in the Crucible of Ministry* (Downers Grove, IL: InterVarsity Press, 2008), 28.

270. Ibid.

271. Discipleship Dynamics LLC, "The Assessment in Detail."

272. Ibid.

273. Ibid.

274. Chandler, *Christian Spiritual Formation*, 84.

275. Discipleship Dynamics LLC, "The Assessment in Detail."

276. Ibid.

277. Clem, *Disciple*, 63.

278. Discipleship Dynamics LLC, "The Assessment in Detail."

279. Chandler, *Christian Spiritual Formation*, 46.

280. Discipleship Dynamics LLC, "The Assessment in Detail."

281. Karen Lawson, "How Do Thoughts and Emotions Affect Health?" Taking Charge of Your Health & Wellbeing, University of Minnesota, 2016, accessed April 7, 2018, http://

www,takingcharge.csh.umn.edu/how-do-thoughts-and-emotions-affect-health.

282. Discipleship Dynamics LLC, "The Assessment in Detail."

283. Eugene E. Carpenter and Philip W. Comfort, *Holman Treasury of Key Bible Verses: 200 Greek and 200 Hebrew Words Defined and Explained* (Nashville, TN: Holman Reference, 2000), 305. Logos Bible Software.

284. Discipleship Dynamics LLC, "The Assessment in Detail."

285. Ibid.

286. Ibid.

287. Ibid.

288. Ibid.

289. Ibid.

290. Ibid.

291. Ibid.

292. John S. Dickerson, *The Great Evangelical Recession: 6 Factors That Will Crash the American Church...and How to Prepare* (Grand Rapids, MI: Baker Books, 2013), 110.

293. Minho Song, "Contextualization and Discipleship: Closing the Gap between Theory and Practice," *Evangelical Review of Theology* 30, no. 3 (2006), 253.

294. Eugene H. Peterson, *A Long Obedience in the Same Direction: Discipleship in an Instant Society* (Downers Grove, IL: InterVarsity Press, 2000), 11.

Chapter 8: Taking the DD Assessment

295. Discipleship Dynamics LLC, "The Assessment in Detail," Discipleship Dynamics, 2016, accessed February 7, 2018, http://discipleshipdynamics.com/about-the-assessment/.

Appendix (Glossary)

296. Discipleship Dynamics LLC, "The Assessment in Detail," Discipleship Dynamics, 2016, accessed February 7, 2018, https://discipleshipdynamics.com/about-the-assessment/.

THE GREAT COMMISSION AND YOU

The Great Commission Jesus gave His disciples in Matthew 28:19-20 exists today as the standard for every believer to follow. "Go and make disciples" then remains the command that should underscore and determine all that believers think and do. There exists, however, a dichotomy between knowing we should be obeying the Great Commission and doing the practical work of it.

This dichotomy can only be resolved by ingraining the discipling DNA of both knowledge and practical application into every believer through specific, measured, time-tested methods found in scripture. How astronomically effective would a disciple-making church be when they are actively focused on bridging the gap between the "knowing" and "doing" aspects of the Great Commission, while fueled by the passion of truly understanding the good news?

The Great Commission and You offers just such a roadmap to help discover, encourage, and put into powerful action, the Great Commission.

How much could your church grow with a congregation educated in the knowledge and practical applications of these powerful methods of evangelism?

About Dr. Stanley Cook

Stan Cook is a husband, father, and proud Papa. He also serves as a pastor, author, speaker, and teacher. Stan is an ordained minister in the Assemblies of God and has over thirty years of practical ministry as a high-school Bible teacher, youth pastor, Christian education pastor, worship leader, interim pastor, bi-vocational pastor, and lead pastor.

Stan and his wife, Heidi, live in Louisville, Kentucky. They have four adult children and three grandchildren.

Stan has earned a Master of Arts degree in Ministerial Leadership from Southeastern University in Lakeland, Florida, and a Doctor of Ministry degree from The Assemblies of God Theological Seminary in Springfield, Missouri.

Stan enjoys reading, playing basketball and golf, and spending time with his wonderful grandchildren.